Weird True Stories

That Sound Made Up

A Collection of Insane-But-True Stories
About Pop Culture, Science, History, And
More To Satisfy Your Curious Brain

(Weird True Stories That Sound Made Up Volume 1)

Kim Miller, **History** Compacted

Table of Contents

4

A Note
From History Compacted

Hi there!

This is Jason Chen, founder of History Compacted. Before you continue your journey to the past, I want to take a quick moment to explain our position on history and the purpose of our books.

To us, history is more than just facts, dates, and names. We see history as pieces of stories that led to the world we know today. Besides, it makes it much more fun seeing it that way too.

That is why History Compacted was created: to tell amazing stories of the past and hopefully inspire you to search for more. After all, history would be too big for any one book. But what each book can give you is a piece of the puzzle to help you get to that fuller picture.

Lastly, I want to acknowledge the fact that history is often told from different perspectives. Depending on the topic and your upbringing, you might agree or disagree with how we present the facts. I understand disagreements are inevitable. That is why with a team of diverse writers, we aim to tell each story from a more neutral perspective. I hope this note can help you better understand our position and goals.

Now without further ado, let your journey to the past begins!

Introduction

Truth is stranger than fiction! This statement by Mark Twain definitely rings true in many ways . From historical stories to urban legends, the stories that we collectively pass down through the ages have a way of transforming into wholly different tales as each new generation gets a hold of them. Sometimes these transformations give them an even stranger and not altogether very accurate air to them. These are just the traditional stories like "Benjamin Franklin and His Lightning" or " Paul Revere's Midnight Ride." These tales may encompass notes of strangeness that keep them being told over and over for centuries. There are many more tales though that are not widely known and even stranger but just as interesting!

From pop culture to science, some stories have remained untold, which is a shame. Like those historical fables we have all heard while sitting in class, these stories deserve to be told. So if you think you had heard some wacky tales before, keep reading. We are sure that you will find more than a few strange stories you have never heard within the tales of this book.

Borrowing Genius!

"**I** want to donate my body to science!" Many great scientists of the past and possibly the modern world feel that they can further science after leaving this world. One of the scientists though that frowned upon this idea was the great Albert Einstein. Albert had seen the limited results from these exams in the past and explicitly asked that his brain not be donated to science.

However, the doctor assigned the autopsy of the celebrated scientist after his passing on April 18, 1955, had a different idea.

That morning, Dr. Thomas Harvey was excited to be chosen to be the one to perform the autopsy. He knew that the scientific genius left behind specific guidelines but deep down inside, he felt it was a waste. Dr. Harvey decided to remove the brain anyway. How would he get the brain out of the lab without people knowing what he was doing? The doctor thought long and hard and crafted a plan that he knew would work.

After carefully removing Einstein's brain, he cut the organ into over two hundred pieces and stashed them in mason jars that he had topped off with celloidin. This procedure would allow him to preserve the pieces of Einstein's brain for further tests later. Of course, once the family took possession of the body, it became apparent that something was missing. Enraged that someone had taken his father's brain, Hans Albert stormed into the doctor's office and demanded that it be returned, but the doctor refused. Dr. Harvey began to explain why it was essential to study his father's brain and through concise and logical argument, he convinced the young Einstein boy to let him do just that.

Unfortunately, though he had received approval from the genius's son, the hospital had a less than favorable response to Harvey's wanton disregard for the protocols. In fact, because he broke the rules, Princeton Hospital had no choice but to let him go. Losing his job would also cost him his marriage, and he would soon find himself packing up to head to the Midwest to escape the consequences of his action, but he didn't leave his treasure behind. For decades, the doctor kept his treasure stored in a cider box in his garage. It wasn't until 1978 that his treasure caught the public eye. Thanks to a dedicated journalist, many research labs eventually reached out to Dr. Harvey for samples.

The bulk of Einstein's brain found its way back to the Penn Medicine Princeton Medical Center and is still kept under lock and key.

Found Guilty Post Mortem!

Once the Roman Empire became the Holy Roman Empire, the reins of power were claimed and seated in some ways to the head of the church, the Pope. One of the duties that the pope had was the ability to name the holy Roman emperor. This power would lead to quite a bit of political maneuvering and, in one case, the trial of a corpse.

At the end of the 9th century, Pope Formosus sat on the papal throne but was very uncertain about who he thought the Roman Emperor should be. At first, the political pressure drove him to name the Duke of Spoleto as the Emperor and then subsequently naming the duke's son to the same position as heir to the throne after the duke's death. After a while, Formosus developed a backbone and stripped the duke's son of the title. He opted to choose one of his good friends, the king of the Eastern Francs. Unfortunately, this choice was short-lived. The new Roman emperor soon found himself paralyzed, and unable to sit on the throne in Rome, he returned to his home country. Not long after this, Formosus died, leaving the papal throne open for his successor Stephen VI.

When Stephen VI took the reins of the papacy, he was left quite a mess. Because of Formosus's uncertainty when it came to who should wear the crown of the holy Roman emperor, Stephen had a lot of work to do. The new Pope immediately acted to place an ally back in the power of the Holy Roman Empire. For this, Stephen looked to Lambert, the Duke of Spoleto's son, who had previously held the crown. To accomplish his goal, Pope Stephen had to show that the previous pope's actions were against the church's edicts and the empire.

This political maneuver meant that he would have to hold court and put the now deceased Formosus on trial. This would, of course, be tricky because Stephen's predecessor had already been dead for nine months. However, this little fact did not stop Stephen from executing his plans, so he ordered the corpse to be dressed and presented in the courtroom so that the trial could proceed. Stephen would appoint one of the deacons to be the voice of the departed pope as he was accused of multiple infractions, including perjury and breaking the laws of the church.

The trial took very little time. Formosus was found guilty. When it came to sentencing of the dearly departed Formosus, Stephen had his body thrown into the Tiber river. This trial sparked many controversies regarding Stephen's reign, but that was not a big deal because his time as pope ended abruptly. At the end of his reign, he was stripped of the title before being imprisoned for his treatment of Pope Formosus' cadaver and the subsequent trial. Stephen didn't last long in prison either; he was found strangled by unknown assailants.

The subsequent Pope Romanus erased the decree of Stephen and had his men drag the Tiber River to retrieve Formosus' body. Once the body was found, Romanus gave it a proper burial, thereby negating the outcome and proclamations of the trial of the pope's cadaver.

This trial would become known as the "Cadaver Synod" and be talked about for centuries amongst the religious scholars of the world.

The South Rises Again

The civil war was a tumultuous time in United States history. With the closing of the war in 1865, the South was pretty much in ruins. The physical rigors of war, as well as the social and economic impact, took a toll on the people. The defeat left most southerners fearful of what the new world would bring. Seeing that the slaves were freed and the man who led the confederacy had been left in jail, they feared retribution from the north. All of this uncertainty spurred some people to consider relocating to different countries.

Seeing the post-war chaos the United States was in, many countries took advantage of this and began trying to lure ex-confederates to migrate to them. Of the countries that saw the benefits of taking in the southerners, many came from Central and South America. Places like Mexico and

Venezuela offered tax breaks and reduced prices on land to entice these individuals to move to their country. But of all the offers that came across the southerners tables, the one from the emperor of Brazil, Dom Pedro II, seemed to have the most traction. The emperor sold the confederates on relocating to Brazil by offering land at twenty-two cents an acre, paying for their transport, temporary lodging, and guaranteeing citizenship upon landing.

Of course, this deal was also intended to benefit the emperor in multiple ways. He would not only get the people that understood new agricultural technologies and practices to farm but also new products that could potentially make more money for the country. At that time, Brazil also had a goal of whitening their society. This policy would be executed by enticing Europeans or those of European descent to settle in Brazil. On top of that, slavery was legal, and this seemed to be a pivotal point in why more than ten thousand ex-confederates took Dom Pedro II up on his offer. These southerners would move and set up six different cities, of which several still exist.

The emperor's offer seemed very enticing when the ex-confederates found their way to immigrating to Brazil. Bur they were greeted with a hot and humid climate that they were not ready for. In the end, many of these ex-confederates wound up moving on to other countries or returning home. There were many different causes of the unsuccessful migration to Brazil, such as soil that was hard to cultivate and a definite language barrier. Even though a large portion of the ex-confederates who set up shop in Brazil left the country, a few hundred stayed, and their families still celebrate the confederacy to this day.

Give Me A Kiss!

It was just another day in 1800s Paris, and like the usual, people were fishing another body out of the Seine river. This time, though, the body was of a young woman that didn't appear to have any markings that would indicate a struggle. The lack of bruises and cuts left the spectators and police to assume she had taken her life.

Dragging suicide victims from the water was nothing that wasn't seen daily, at least two hundred people on average were pulled from the muddy waters of the Paris River. In fact, it was such a common occurrence that Paris had a division specifically for this called the River Police.

At this time in history, when a body was unable to be identified, they were displayed in the morgue window. This practice would allow someone strolling the streets of Paris the ability to recognize them. Once this happened the unknown corpse would be able to have a decent burial. No one identified her so her story was left to the imagination of poets and artists alike.

Her face was destined for fame though, but it all started with a simple pathologist and his infatuation with this unknown woman's beautiful face. Feeling that her face was remarkably peaceful and elegant, the pathologist decided to make a plaster cast of her face. From this cast, others were made, and soon her face was in many of the fashionable homes throughout Europe. The death mask of this unfortunate soul became an inspiration for many poems and stories where the artists crafted an identity for this young lady.

The cast survived for several decades before it found its final home as the face of "Resusci Anne," the infamous CPR doll. When mouth-to-mouth resuscitation was invented, a few doctors worried about the health of the medical students learning the practice as they seemed to be hurting one another as they were learning this new procedure. One of these doctors was Archer Gordon, and he, along with another doctor, decided they needed a tool that the students could practice on that wouldn't get hurt. So they reached out to toymaker Asmund Laerdal, who had once seen the death mask of this young girl and decided it would be the perfect face for his new mannequin.

This toymaker's company still makes these mannequins, and since more than three hundred million individuals have been trained in CPR, this tragic figure has become the most kissed girl in the world.

Anybody Got A Light?

After the overthrowing of the Batista regime in Cuba, Fidel Castro took the reins of the country. Over the next several years, this Cuban president established a communist regime that would leave the United States on edge.

The U.S. was the beacon of democracy and amid the Cold War with Russia, so having a communist government so close seemed dangerous. Another factor that may have led the U.S. government to prompt the CIA into developing plans to remove Castro from power by any means necessary was the unusually close relationship between the Cuban and Russian governments.

These plans included state-sanctioned assassination attempts. In fact, there have allegedly been over six hundred different attempts to take Castro out over his long reign. Of course, the conventional means to assassinate a victim was enough, but the CIA didn't want to take their chances with Castro. It was time to think outside of the box.

The CIA wanted to try and get as close as possible to the communist leader, so they decided to include intimate details from the personal life of the dictator into these plans. They took under advisement the things that Castro enjoyed, including luxuries like cigars, scuba diving, seashells, and even swimming. Several of the plots, though, centered around his infamous cigar habit. One attempt that the CIA tried was to poison Castro's cigar with LSD. They dipped his cigars in the drug and hoped he would become unhinged on television and put a dent in his reputation.

Of all the plots having to do with his cigar, the one that seems the most unbelievable was the one with the exploding cigar. The CIA had worked hard to craft a cigar that had explosive properties. Finally, in 1960, they successfully got an operative in close enough quarters to Castro to poison a box of his favorite cigars. After receiving the special package, it seems that this person went missing along with the box of cigars.

Whether Castro caught wind of the plot, or the person got cold feet, we will never know. One thing is for sure—the cigars never made it to the dictator.

Wrong Turn

Tensions were high in the Balkan region during the early part of the 1900s. The Austro-Hungarian empire had taken charge of several smaller countries, claiming them as their own, and creating unrest among the native populace. By 1909, the empire had complete control of Bosnia Herzegovina, and the Serbian nationalists were not happy with this situation.

To improve the Serbian relations and ensure that the military was ready for whatever was coming, the Austro-Hungarian emperor sent Archduke Franz Ferdinand and his wife to visit Sarajevo in June 1914. Little did they know that this was going to lead to much more than a simple military inspection.

The Young Bosnians, a nationalist student-formed organization, wanted to stand up for themselves. But they were not as aggressive as they wanted to be, so the young college students formed a partnership with the Black Hand, a much more militaristic terrorist organization that had ties with the Serbian military.

Ferdinand, fully aware of the tensions and danger present, went ahead with the emperor's plan to visit Sarajevo. This visit, of course, gave these young nationalists a prime opportunity to send a message to the Austro-Hungarian government. It was the perfect time to assassinate the archduke, and the publicity attached to his visit made this goal even more accessible.

To ensure enough people were there to celebrate the archduke's arrival; the travel route was published in newspapers. Eager to make an impact and show that the empire cared about their annexed countries, Ferdinand hopped in his car early on June 28, 1914. He and his wife planned to drive in an open convertible motorcade visible to their subjects and wave to them, building a better public image for the royal family. This plan meant that they were open to attack, which is precisely what the Young Bosnians planned to do.

The seven young men obtained explosive devices intending to toss them inside the car as the motorcade passed. The weather and concerns about the couple's safety led to the archduke, and his wife driving with the top up. This last-minute decision didn't stop the attempt, though, as Nedeljko Cabrinovic still lobbed one of the bombs at the car.

It bounced off the roof and rolled under the vehicle behind the car containing the archduke. The explosive went off and injured two soldiers in that car. So it seemed that the assassination attempt had failed, but there were still casualties.

The archduke was concerned and felt terrible that two of his soldiers had been injured. So once the meetings were done, Archduke Ferdinand insisted that he wanted to visit the wounded soldiers. On high alert, the motorcade driver cautiously drove down the streets and, trying to find alternative routes, turned down a dead-end alley where one of the members of the young nationalist group, Gavrilo Princip had found cover.

Princip saw an opportunity to finish what they had started earlier that morning and drew his pistol, firing multiple shots at Ferdinand and his wife, killing them both.

It seems that the archduke was unable to change his fate. His death altered the face of Europe and the rest of the world marking the beginning of WWI.

Sound The Alarms

America was rocked when the Japanese attacked on December 9, 1941. So rocked that it catapulted the country into WWII. This attack caused many Americans to worry that more strikes would be executed on the mainland, which brought a level of hysteria never seen before. After the attack, many military personnel swore they spotted foreign vessels in the waters off the coast of the United States.

On February 23, 1942, these concerns were realized when a Japanese submarine off the Santa Barbara coast surfaced and launched several artillery shells at a refinery and oil field. No one was injured, but it put everyone on high alert and set the stage for the battle of Los Angeles.

Two days later, in the early hours of February 25th, a young military radar man yelled to his commanding officer to come closer to the radar station as he thought that he had seen something. It seemed that an enemy vessel had appeared on the radar just one hundred twenty miles from Los Angeles. Already on edge from the previous submarine attack, the radar man quickly sounded air raid sirens and sent word for a citywide blackout. Once these safety protocols had been executed, it took almost no time for the troops to find their way to the antiaircraft guns. The troops swept the fast beams of their large searchlights, looking for the enemy aircraft. An hour later, someone spotted an unidentified object in the sky—the guns in Santa Monica released a barrage into the sky, hoping to take the enemy down. As the guns blazed in Santa Monica, other defenses on the coast began to take up arms as well. Soon, the sky was filled with searchlights and orange explosions.

The battle yielded no definitive proof that there was actually enemy aircraft in the skies over Los Angeles. The sky lit up for an hour, and when the troops were called to stand down, there had been fourteen hundred rounds of anti-aircraft ammunition shot into the California skies. As the military and citizens of Los Angeles worked hard to clean up the debris and destruction caused by the battle the previous night, many pieces of contradictory information began to leak.

It seems as if the military had no real clue of what happened. Some sources said a weather balloon was released into the sky, which caused a blip to appear on the radar while other military officials swore that enemy planes were buzzing the city. In the end, no one really knows what happened at the Battle of Los Angeles.

Many conspiracies have been floated around though, including that the unidentified objects in the sky were actually of extraterrestrial origin. What happened in the skies over Los Angeles on February 25, 1942? The truth is no one may ever know.

A Little Inspiration

Sir Isaac Newton was born in 1642, close to the English city of Grantham. Growing up the son of a farmer, Isaac had to work hard and eventually found his way into the halls of Cambridge University. He studied at this iconic college for four years until the school was closed due to a pandemic associated with the bubonic plague. Once the doors of the school shut, Isaac packed his bags up and went home.

This tragic event actually ended up being a godsend because this is where Newton found his inspiration. During the day, Isaac liked to sit and stare into the orchards that surrounded his home. It was here that the infamous apple story came into being. Many children in school learned about the apple that fell on his head, which inspired him to look into the scientific reason why this happened, eventually leading to Newton formulating the Universal Law of Gravity.

However magical that story is, there is no proof it is real. All that matters is that Newton was inspired to investigate why the apple fell straight down and not sideways or upwards. Because of this, he was able to publish his first principle in 1687; the famous Law of Attraction. He also included his Three Laws of Motion within the pages of this publication.

One of the strangest and most interesting things about this story is that it led many historians to look for the species of the tree that Newton was looking for. With a story as important as this, the historians wanted to get all the facts straight. Many historians feel that it is the flower of Kent apple tree planted in Woolsthorpe Manor Newton's family home around 1650. Unfortunately, this tree was damaged in 1816, due to a significant storm, and even crazier is that this original tree still stands today.

Burying A Classic

Today, when you go to an electronics or video game store, you can choose between multiple consoles. But back in the early 1980s, there was only one, and it dominated the market. Every kid wanted an Atari, and it didn't take Atari long to realize that they could capitalize on the popularity of certain movies and franchises. In fact, they had one of the most successful collaborations when they adapted *Raiders of the Lost Ark* to their console.

So, it's not surprising that in 1982, when Steven Spielberg wrapped up his film *E.T.*, he thought it would be a good idea to reach out to the company and see what they could do with it. Atari jumped at the chance to work on adapting a Steven Spielberg film and shelled out twenty-million dollars to do so. It was such an enormous expenditure, this would leave Steve Ross, who was the president of Atari at the time, having to sell, at the bare minimum, four million copies of the game to even make a profit on the title.

The previous film adaption had taken ten months, but because Spielberg and the company had made their deal in July; the designers would only have five weeks to finish the project. Pushing hard and working for his team even harder, Howard Scott Warshaw completed the game and even got Spielberg to sign off on it. Unfortunately, despite the excitement surrounding the game, it was soon evident that five months was not enough time to develop a great game with a fantastic story.

In fact, as more and more people purchased the game, more complaints began emerging about the gameplay and some significant glitches, including the fact that *E.T.* tended to get stuck in holes. In the end, the game sold two and a half million copies, which made it more successful than people thought it could be with all the glitches.

But what does a video game company do with excess video games that will never be sold? If you're Atari, you drive them into the middle of the desert in Alamogordo, New Mexico, and bury them.

For years, Atari, tried to keep the dumping quiet but eventually journalists uncovered it and revealed this truth to the world.

The internet, of course, kept it going, and in 2014, documentary filmmaker Zack Penn returned to the site and excavated hundreds of copies of the game still sealed in their packages.

Spark Of Interest

Many kids across the globe have been told the story of Benjamin Franklin flying his kite in an electrical storm. The truth of this story is not nearly as exciting as the one described, and it wasn't even as historically significant as some may make it seem.

Benjamin Franklin did not discover electricity, nor did he figure out that electricity could be derived from lightning. In 1752, the illustrious kite and storm experiment that supposedly shocked the scientists when he was electrocuted by the lightning hitting a key attached to the kite took place. This experiment's results were straightforward, actually, and when Franklin touched the kite, he got a little bit of a static shock. However, another scientist had already proven the correlation between electricity and lightning a month earlier in Europe, so it seems redundant for Franklin to do this experiment.

Perhaps the story was combined with another tale of Franklin getting the shock of his life. In fact, there was a time an experiment that Franklin did experience electrocution. It wasn't nearly as glamorous, though, because he was trying to tenderize and cook a turkey. Ready to make dinner one night in 1749, Franklin attached wires to a turkey and prepared to utilize this power in a whole new way. Unfortunately for Benjamin Franklin, he accidentally touched two electrical components called Leyden jars and was electrocuted into unconsciousness.

Once Franklin had awoken from his unconsciousness, the onlookers of this incident explained to him what had happened. It seems that Franklin didn't remember, but when he received the shock, his body shook, and then unconsciousness took over. Of course, Franklin didn't walk away unscathed. He had numbness in several of his extremities and was sore for a few days after. Still, he definitely formulated some hypotheses on what happens to humans when they are electrocuted.

It's Poison!

In 1920, with the ratification by Congress of the 18th amendment, prohibition became law. Prohibition made drinking and serving alcohol illegal in all fifty states, but just because it became law doesn't mean the parties stopped. Because of this, many people took to running a black market economy where bootleggers helped supply alcohol to undercover bars known as speakeasies. With the realization that the federal law hadn't stopped anything, the government knew they had to take alternative actions to ensure that people were not still enjoying alcohol. The alcohol that the bootleggers were dispersing tended to be crafted using methanol, which was already a toxic chemical. Taking the cue from this, the government decided that they would up the toxicity of chemicals used in this process.

This law would stay in place for thirteen years. During those years, the federal government would change the guidelines for chemical companies when it came to adding toxic chemicals to select substances. These additions included things like kerosene, cadmium, zinc, mercury salts, nicotine, formaldehyde, and quinine, to name a few. On top of this, the Treasury Department made it mandatory for chemical formulas to include ten percent methyl alcohol. Adding all these chemicals to compounds used in alcohol distillation meant that the alcohol produced was more potent and, conversely, more deadly.

Even with all these extra measures, people still wanted to have a little adult beverage every now and then, and because of this, many U.S. citizens died. Though the records are unclear about exactly how many, there have been quotes of numbers up to ten thousand people who died from the poisonous chemicals used by the government to make people stop drinking.

Bah Humbug!

Christmas has changed over the centuries so much that it might be hard to believe, but four hundred years ago, people wanted to get rid of Christmas. Who were these people? The people that had a target on the December holiday were none other than the very strict Puritans. It may seem strange for a Christian organization to actually take aim at one of their main holidays, but the Puritans had their reasons. The Christmas of yesteryear was not the friendly, family-oriented holiday the modern world celebrates but was still very tied to the holidays Pagan solstice roots. This fact meant that there was not only drinking and gambling at Christmas but also some pretty raucous behavior. All of which the Puritans felt were counter-intuitive to the Christian teachings.

Because of this symbiotic relationship with the religions of the old world, the Puritans of the Massachusetts Bay colony took drastic measures. In May of 1659, the legislature of this colony got together and banned the holiday altogether. Along with this ban, they set a fine of five shillings for anyone brave enough to continue the celebration. The ban lasted for twenty-two years.

In 1681, after receiving extensive pressure to maintain England's law, the puritan legislation repealed the law. Even with the repeal of this law, most Massachusetts Bay colonists, who were still devout Puritans, opted out of the festivities.

In fact, the holiday didn't see a significant revival in that part of the United States until the mid-1800s, when authors like Charles Dickens made the holiday popular once again.

Punch In The Gut

Illusionists and magicians were one of the biggest entertainment pools throughout the 1900s. People like Harry Houdini and David Copperfield became synonymous with death-defying and unimaginable feats performed in front of audiences.

Even though more big names came later in the 1900s, most of these illusionists and magicians all had one hero: the Hungarian-born Harry Houdini. Harry Houdini performed some death-defying feats throughout his career, yet his death is still quite the mystery. This mystery is partly exacerbated because the magician himself was known to overlook pain to execute his performances.

In late October of 1926, Houdini sat in a dressing room along with three students who wanted to meet him preparing for his Montreal exhibition. Among the students, one of the students had a question they had been dying to ask. The young student was very interested in Houdini's claim that he could take the most brutal blow to his stomach simply by tightening the muscles. Houdini went on about how this was true, and so the young student asked if they could test that theory. Of course, not wanting to be called to the carpet, Houdini agreed to allow the student to punch him in the stomach. The student stood up and before Houdini could flex his muscles the student preceded to punch the illustrious magician in the stomach several times. For the rest of the day, Houdini told everyone he was feeling fine.

Unfortunately, later in the evening, he began to have severe stomach pains. Worried that something was wrong, his doctor took his temperature, which came in at one hundred four degrees Fahrenheit. The doctor was concerned but Houdini refused to be treated as the show must go on. However, it soon became apparent that he could not continue his show and wound up being rushed to the hospital. Once there, the doctors diagnosed him with a ruptured appendix and removed it.

This performance would be the final curtain for Houdini. Though the doctors had removed the ruptured appendix, he soon developed peritonitis and passed away on Halloween of 1926.

Of course, no one will ever know the exact cause of his death as there was no autopsy done. Some conspiracy theorists believe that he was poisoned because of his very vocal opinion of the spiritualists of the time. After his mother passed, Houdini drifted towards spiritualism to contact her. But in doing this he discovered that most spiritualists of the time used illusions and trickery to con people out of their money. Once he learned this, he made it is personal mission to bring these practices to light and this made many spiritualists angry, which is why this theory gained traction among certain circles.

Though nothing can be proven, the death of Harry Houdini remains a strange tale and one filled with mystery.

Scouting A Location

Every urban legend known to man has some basis in reality.

Over the years, there have been many urban legends and rumors about everything that went on in the Third Reich during WWII and beyond. One of these rumors was the longstanding story that the Germans were attempting to build a secret military base in the Antarctic. Karl Donitz, one of those convicted during the Nuremberg trials, pretty much copped to the idea that the rumor was true but never came to fruition.

Though there were significant resources expended on a project looking to acquire natural resources from that region, Hitler was beginning his buildup of the German economy to sustain his future war intentions by 1936. One of the most essential things in the economy and for natural resources were animal fats. Animal fat created everything from milk and cheese to cleaning supplies and paint. The fear was that the German economy might run short during the war.

Hitler began to think of inventive ways to find animal fats. At the time, whale oil was still used to make a lot of different products, including margarine, but most of Germany's whale oil came from Norway. Knowing that this may not be a reliable source, Hitler decided to build a fleet of whaling ships.

Two years later, the whaling fleet was ready, so in 1938, Captain Alfred Ritscher and eighty-two sailors set off for Antarctica. Over the next several months, the team photographed and mapped the coastline of Antarctica. Once this was done, they returned home to relay the information they had found. Though they had done a lot of hard work, the Third Reich eventually focused on areas other than the whaling industry.

When the war ended, the expedition proved to come with an unintended benefit. It was revealed that they had mapped sixteen percent more of Antarctica and also discovered the mid-Atlantic Ridge.

Never Gonna Give Up

It is well known that the Japanese military is highly disciplined. During WWII, this reputation was often talked about in the form of fanaticism. It should be no surprise that once the war was over, several of these dedicated men remained at large fighting a war that had come to its conclusion.

In September of 1945, the Japanese surrendered to the allied forces. The Japanese forces had found their way onto most Pacific islands by then, so the word took a little time to get to some of the more remote deployments. This widespread deployment meant that for several months after (years actually), there were minor skirmishes throughout many of the small islands.

One example of these minor skirmishes that continued happened in December of the same year. Sakae Oba, the commanding officer of a deployed forced, surrendered in Saipan with his forty-six men. They had fought bravely and held out as long as they could but eventually had to buckle to the U.S. forces that had landed on the island. This small band of Japanese soldiers were the first of the forces that refused to actually lay down their arms. Incidents like this would go on through the 40s and 50s.

One of the most famous soldiers from that war who held on to the battle, Hiroo Onoda would finally emerge from the jungle in 1974. The soldier had lived and continued the struggle in the thick Philippine bush for almost three decades. Being an intelligence officer in charge of guerrilla warfare on Lubang island, he and his cohorts refused to believe the news and kept fighting.

When asked why he and his three subordinates continued, Onada said that there was no way the allied forces would trick him into losing honor by surrendering. When the government of Japan dropped flyers trying to persuade Onada to give up, he thought it was an American trick and continued with his assignment.

He eventually realized that the war was over and surrendered. This dedicated soldier passed in 2014. Many other Japanese soldiers allegedly refused to give up even up to the 2000's.

Talking Through Your Teeth

There are many urban legends when it comes to presidents and other historical figures. Perhaps one of the most famous is that George Washington sported a fantastic set of wooden teeth. This story, however, is simply a myth!

George Washington suffered from problems with his teeth throughout his life. He began losing teeth in his early twenties, and by the time the Revolutionary War came along, he was already donning his first set of dentures. There is also a rumor that he had an extraordinary surgery where teeth from other people were implanted into his mouth. Some even say there were quite a few of these teeth that were purchased from his own slaves.

Even if Washington did not have this surgery and went instead with a special pair of dentures a dentist made for him, when he was sworn in as the first president of the United States in 1789, he had absolutely no original teeth left.

The teeth he went into the office with were made of ivory, brass, and gold. The ivory, which was the overall base of the teeth, was very hard to keep up without consistent cleaning, and so oftentimes, his dentures would look very stained. This stain may be why many people thought he was wearing teeth made of wood.

It's The End Of The World

Edmund Halley, English astronomer and meteorologist, took Newton's gravitational theories and charted out paths of more than two dozen comets in 1705. His theory was that you could predict their appearance in the sky if you could only figure out how long it took for them to orbit around the sun.

Because of his dedication and scientific prowess, Halley was able to inspire other astronomers, and one of those was a French gentleman named Nicolas-Louis de Lacaille. Using the research left behind by Halley, this French astronomer charted the night skies waiting to see if his idol's theories were true. By 1758, Halley was finally proven to be right when one of his comets streaked across the night's sky. This celestial body would become the infamous comet known as

Halley's Comet that would cause a panic on its return in 1910.

The scientific discipline of astronomy had been advancing quickly over the 1500s and 1600s, and with more knowledge came more superstitions. Because people now understood more about the objects in the night sky and what they actually were, it made the universe so much bigger and, therefore, more intimidating.

By the time the 1900s came around, most people had shaken off these fears of comets being an omen of bad things to come, and instead, people thought that it could be the cause of mass extinction. As the time neared for the comet to appear, many stories began to circulate about the doomsday that Halley's Comet would bring with it. These stories range from the comet causing a shift in the Pacific basin to dangerous gases that would wipe out humanity. French astronomer Camille Flammarion would latch onto this last idea and incite panic globally.

Over the previous few decades, many astronomers had studied these comets using scientific processes such as spectroscopy. This research led to the realization that Halley's Comet's tail was made of cyanogen gas.

Flammarion was concerned about what would happen to this gas upon entering the atmosphere. His theory was that as it entered the atmosphere, the chemical reaction would cause it to begin poisoning the air and, in turn, every person on the planet. He was not afraid to share this theory with everyone who would listen, including media outlets.

One of the biggest media outlets, the New York Times, picked up the story and ran with it. Unfortunately, this would cause panic through the streets, and people began to prepare for doomsday. Everyone was looking to protect themselves from the oncoming doom, so they started buying gas masks and preparing their homes for the impending end of the world. There were even people who took advantage of this and began marketing things like anti-comet pills (which turned out to be sugar pills).

As it turns out, Halley's Comet would streak across the night sky like it always did, leaving the world pretty much unchanged.

Celestial Fireflies!

In the late 50s and early 60s, the U.S. space program was very much a focus for the government. John Glenn was chosen as one of the first astronauts to head into space in 1959. As part of the "Mercury Seven," he was destined to go down in history. His career would include the moon landing, being the first American who orbited the earth, and several other feats. But one of the most well-known and strange stories happened during his 1962 mission into space. Set to orbit the earth three times in a ship known as Friendship 7, Glenn would see something, at the time, which was unexplainable.

The mission had just begun, and as he started his first orbit around the earth he saw something strange floating outside the window of his capsule. He quickly radioed NASA and reported what he saw in detail. He described the items as luminous stars that surrounded the capsule. As he tried to explain what they looked like further, he eventually came upon just the right adjective. Glenn, a respected and logical military man, deemed these specks of brilliant-light fireflies. They floated in the air around his capsule, and he began to pound on the walls to see if he could get the fireflies to move.

The scientists on the ground started to worry that this was a malfunction with the space capsule. Others began to think that Glenn was in some sort of medical emergency. There were those who believed that it was more of a celestial or even, dare they say, extraterrestrial experience.

It took a year and a whole different mission for the scientists at NASA to solve this mystery. As Aurora 7 began its orbital flight around the earth, another astronaut, Scott Carpenter, reported seeing something as well. This time, the astronauts also saw the luminescent particles floating through space, though they looked like snowflakes.

This difference of perception was what sparked the scientists determining what John Glenn's fireflies actually were. It turns out that he was seeing condensation that had frozen and broken off from the outside of the capsule. As these particles moved through different areas that had different temperatures, they radiated different colors.

The mystery of John Glenn and his fireflies was solved, even if it wasn't as exciting as an extra-terrestrial encounter.

Death Of A Poet

In October of 1849, things were looking pretty good for Edgar Allan Poe. Not only was he a celebrated author and bringing in large crowds when it came to his readings, but he had finally found love. Before marrying his true love, Edgar decided to go on a business trip that had him traveling from Richmond to Philadelphia and then to New York. However, this trip would be cut short when he reached Baltimore; he suddenly vanished.

A week went by before he was finally found. Joseph Walker, a huge fan of the author, found him in Gunner's Hall, a pretty famous tavern, on October 3rd. The gentleman would describe how he found Poe in a letter to one of Poe's acquaintances. Apparently, Poe was disheveled and in a delirious state, lying in a gutter when the gentleman offered to help him. The first thing Joseph Walker asked was if Poe knew anybody in the area, and of course, he gave the young man a name. Once Poe's acquaintance was contacted, he took the incoherent author into his care.

Seeing the state of his friend, the gentleman immediately took Poe to the Washington College Hospital. Poe was admitted there, and was attended to by Dr. John Moran. The records are pretty sparse but based on what can be found the doctor had him placed in a windowless room for observation. Poe would spend his last days in an incoherent and belligerent state.

On October 7, 1849, four days after being found, the celebrated author succumbed to his health issues. It is reported that his last words were, "Lord, help my poor soul."

Since that very day, there has been mystery surrounding Edgar Allan Poe's death. Where had he been that week? And why, when he appeared, was he in such a horrible condition? According to the records, his cause of death was phrenitis, which was the terminology used for someone who passed from an alcohol or drug overdose.

Though this is the official record, many have other theories. Some medical physicians thought maybe he had succumbed to rabies or even carbon monoxide or heavy metal poisoning. There are even some thought that his death resulted from someone torturing him for that week and slowly beating him to death. Because of the poor records from those days, the truth may never be known.

Abandoned At Sea

There are hundreds of stories about groups of people disappearing, never to be seen again. Several of these stories are very famous, like the tale of the Roanoke Colony and the Mary Celeste. The story of the Mary Celeste, though, is maybe the most bizarre and has never been solved to this day.

In November 1872, the Brigantine vessel left New York harbor with a destination set for Genoa, Italy. Captaining this long voyage was Benjamin S. Briggs, who brought along his wife, his daughter, and eight crew members. In the cargo hold of the ship, they transported seventeen hundred barrels of crude alcohol. Just short of a month later, this vessel would be found floating in the open seas by the captain of a British ship, David Morehouse.

Catching sight of the ship floating aimlessly through the sea, the captain and his men docked next to the boat and boarded the Mary Celeste. Taking in every detail, the captain only saw minor damage to the sails, and the hold was filled with several feet of water. Along with this, they noted that a lifeboat and all the navigational instruments were nowhere to be found. When they made it to the cargo hold, the cargo was still there though. Working their way further into the ship, they found all of the food and water that the crew and captain would have needed for the voyage were still stored in the galley.

The captain and his crew made their way carefully through each of the vessels compartment and finally came upon captain Briggs's log. Morehouse found the last entry, dated nine days and five hundred miles from where he had found the ship, but there did not seem to be anything of consequence that could solve why the captain and the crew disappeared without a trace.

Briggs, his family, and his crew were never seen again. Because of the state of the ship, this mystery has prevailed. There were no signs of any reason for this group of people to abandon the vessel, leading to a long list of theories. These stories range from mutiny to assaults by a giant octopus.

There are even some that think it may have had to do with alien abduction.

Because no one was ever found and there was nothing left in the logs, this weird but true story will continue to captivate people for decades to come.

Angel Of Mons

In the fall of 1914, the world found itself at war. The Germans took advantage of the unstable climate in Europe after the assassination of archduke Franz Ferdinand in Sarajevo, and began to expand their empire not just to the east but also to the west to keep the French at bay. They would have to go through the British Expeditionary Force (BEF) that set up a defensive line in Belgium to reach France.

Though there were more Germans, the BEF was more experienced when it came to wartime. The two forces clashed at Mons, and after a bloody conflict, the British troops were able to force the Germans to retreat. This was a glorious battle, but it was the story that came out of this skirmish that makes this British victory such a strange tale.

According to one tale that spread through England, their British forces were aided by a band of angels that came from the heavens with flaming swords to stand beside the British forces and smote the Germans. This story gained momentum because of media and religious fervor.

The truth is that this story was a fictionalized tale that was crafted well after the battle had ended. An author had published a story envisioning medieval archers appearing to help fight the German forces at Mons in the evening news, a popular newspaper at the time.

Having caught wind of this tale, many people began to discuss a celestial or heavenly entity present at the battle. A year later, an article was released in newspapers and magazines where two soldiers that had fought at the battle claimed to have seen angels fighting during the combat.

Since then, there has been a mystery of whether there really was divine assistance during the critical battle or not.

Attack Of The Mad Gasser

When people hear tales of strange figures and unexplained attacks, they picture major cities as the home of these stories. But in the fall of 1944, a small town in Illinois called Mattoon would forever go down in the annals of weird stories. September 1, 1944, started like any other day, but by the end of that day this small Illinois town would see the beginning of what would turn out to be something that sent them into a panic.

It started that evening in one home, where a mother and child began to smell a sweet odor filling their house. It didn't take long for the mother to find herself paralyzed, and this frightening occurrence was also accompanied by the appearance of a prowler around the family home. Something this strange in a small city quickly gained attention and a story was published in the local newspaper.

The published story further sensationalized the mystery and helped prevent more attacks from happening.

To lend credit to this claim, the journalist interviewed another couple that on August 31st had also detected a similar smell. In this instance, the wife's legs had become paralyzed, and her husband had begun to vomit almost immediately. In an attempt to grab readers attentions, the journalist dubbed the events as "The Mad Gasser Attacks."

Over the following several weeks, more victims came forward. On September 5th, a woman concerned that she may have heard something outside her home, went outside to investigate and found a wet cloth lying on the ground. Suspicious, she grabbed it, and as the smell wafted towards her, she collapsed unconscious. This attack was followed by eight other individuals coming forward claiming that their home had been attacked by the mad gasser. As more victims came forward and the case became wider, the FBI was finally called in to begin its investigation.

On September 13th, twenty more individuals came forward claiming to have been victims of the Mad Gasser.

The FBI and the local police were perplexed and continued investigating. In spite of the fact many of them were sure that these attacks were simply hysteria caused by the emissions being emitted from nearby industrial plants. .

However, after the last twenty attacks, the Mad Gasser never struck again. Whether it was one individual or a group of criminals who viciously attacked families and their homes in this small town is a still mystery. No one was ever caught, and according to the doctors, who examined the victims, there was no trace of any chemical that could have caused these illnesses.

Like with most weird stories, there are always rumors and theories that attempt to solve the unknown.

A Sleepy Sickness

There have been many global epidemics and pandemics over the centuries. Through science and medicine, most of these diseases have been either cured or studied enough that the causes of that disease were negated. However, despite the best effort of doctors and scientist around the world, there is still one sickness that spread across the globe without a cure. Unfortunately, it is not just a tale told to scare people but something that really happened in the early 1900s.

In 1916, doctors began to have patients come in with unusual symptoms like drowsiness, tremors, and psychosis, baffling physicians. Soon more and more patients sharing the same symptoms were arriving. Between 1916 and the late 1920s, this epidemic remained vigilant and ended up killing almost a million people. Many of those that survived found themselves unable to live life as they had before, with most spending the rest of their lives as invalids.

Through the entire epidemic, doctors continued to struggle with finding the causes of this disease. They were sure that the disease was attacking the brain, so it was named Encephalitis lethargica. Other than this information, everything else was a mystery to them. But then, just as quickly as this disease had reared its ugly head, it disappeared. Even though the disease had disappeared, it still left a wake of devastation in its path and remained a mystery for decades.

Just when everyone thought the disease was gone, the mysterious disease suddenly reappeared in the 1990s. With the advancements in technology and medicine, a group of doctors figured out the cause of this terrible disease.

These doctors noticed that the twenty victims diagnosed with this disease all came in with one significant symptom in common: a sore throat. Through deduction, the doctors figured out that a form of streptococcus caused the epidemic that had caused so much trouble in the early 1900s. Even with this knowledge, there is still no cure for Encephalitis lethargica, which seems quite odd to most people.

Hopefully, one day, with the help of modern advancements in medicine, we will be rid of the fear that this disease will pop up again.

Vampires In New England

In the early 1700s, New England was hit by a sweeping deadly disease that wiped out entire families. This disease left the afflicted with pale skin and sunken eyes. To reduce the panic, doctors tried to explain that these were just physical symptoms attached to the actual disease. Despite doctors best efforts to dispel these myths though, the superstitious people of New England decided that what they had on their hands was clear—this was a vampire epidemic.

This "vampire epidemic" hysteria spread beyond New England, with several hysteria outbreaks occurring in countries across Europe as well. Nobody understood the disease, much less how to treat it, and so panic ensued.

As the vampire panic swept the eastern seaboard of the U.S., many unbelievable stories spread with it, with one of the most famous being the case of Mercy Brown in Exeter, Rhode Island. Mercy was one among the many members of her family who were diagnosed with consumption and later on passed away. As more members of the Brown family began to succumb to this disease, rumors began to fly speculating that maybe the reason why so many of the Brown family were passing away was because there was something more sinister involved—a vampire.

With so many town members whispering behind his back, Mercy's father, who had survived the disease, opted to allow local officials to exhume his family's bodies. Officials started with the most recent member of the family that had died, and that was George's daughter Mary. Instead of burying this young woman in the ground, the family chose an above-ground crypt. This decision would only serve to further the panic surrounding a vampire being present in the village. As officials entered the vault, the body with little to no decomposition still looked flushed as if she was going to sit up to greet them at any moment.

Seeing this, Georges's fellow Exeter townspeople were sure that Mercy Brown, the first to pass, had to be a vampire. Soon though, George's son Edwin also came down with consumption, and the villagers came up with a way they could cure him. They removed Mercy's heart and burned it, mixing the ashes with water. They then had Edwin drink it and claimed that the Browns were no longer in danger from their undead family member.

Two months later, Edwin passed from the disease, and with him, the Brown family was freed of this curse. The locals claimed it was because of their cure! In the end, it was actually a tuberculosis outbreak combined with several other lung diseases that most historians think was the culprit.

Because of the unique circumstances of this story and its similarity to one of the scenarios in Bram Stoker's famous book, Dracula, some feel that this case was an inspiration to the Irish writer among the plethora of other inspirations he used to craft the lassi novel

Mary Tuft And Her Fluffle

The world is full of beautiful mysteries that keep us all guessing, but sometimes those mysteries are nothing more than a hoax. One of these hoaxes is the story of the woman who gave birth to rabbits. In September of 1726, a local doctor was called to assist in a home delivery. Little did they know, this would cause a stir throughout England.

John Howard arrived at the home of Mary Toft and found her right in the middle of giving birth to some pretty strange "babies." As he assisted the woman, he delivered things like cat legs and several baby rabbits. The news about a human woman giving birth to rabbit kittens spread and soon enough the story also caught the attention of the king himself. Interested in this mysterious case, the king sent one of his doctors to look and see what was happening. The royal surgeon arrived at just the right time to see Miss Toft give birth to the fifteenth rabbit.

It may seem strange to modern people, but these two highly educated doctors were taken in by the fact that Mary Toft was delivering rabbits. To explain this odd occurrence, the doctors used a theory called Maternal Impression. These doctors felt that Mary had come across a rabbit that startled her during her pregnancy, which is why she had begun to give birth to rabbits.

However, some other doctors found that this was ridiculous and that the human body would not be able to develop the organs and everything that rabbits would need to live. There were also autopsies done on several of the dead animals, which were found to contain food in their stool. This odd occurrence really confused the two doctors, so Howard felt he needed to take this woman to London to be examined by the medical experts there. Once they arrived, the media circus began.

More and more people were captivated by the story, which caused them to want to get up close and see this amazing miracle. Local papers were amongst these spectators who wanted to get to the bottom of what was going on. Their coverage spread the story further and further, but once the woman and her doctor arrived in London, the births stopped. This abrupt stop to the deliveries began to raise suspicions that perhaps this was all a hoax, but the final straw that broke that camel's back was when someone was caught trying to sneak a rabbit into Mary Toft's room. After this occurrence, the doctor began to question the births himself and threatened the woman with surgery.

As the threat of going under the knife became real, the woman broke down and confessed that she had been hoping that this hoax would be able to bring her money. She also explained that she had inserted the animal body parts into her body through her vagina.

Mary Toft may have not been giving birth to babies, but she certainly created an interest in the strange and mysterious for many.

In The Blink Of An Eye

In 1890, Britain and Germany signed a treaty that basically laid out borders of influence between these two mega powers in East Africa, Tanzania, and Zanzibar. The Heligoland-Zanzibar treaty gave control of Tanzania to Germany and Zanzibar to the British. This treaty allowed Britain to make Zanzibar a protectorate of the empire and place its own ruler on the throne. The British chose Hamad bin Thuwaini, a staunch British supporter, to be the ruler of this land in 1893. For three years, this region was peaceful, but in August of 1896, the British ruler passed away under suspicious circumstances.

With the Sultan dead, his nephew, Khalid bin Barghash, stepped up and proclaimed himself in charge. However, the protection treaty that had been signed placed all new appointments to the country's head under the control of the British consul. The new Sultan chose to stand his ground and stay holed up in the palace with approximately over twenty-five hundred men.

The British responded by moving several ships and hundreds of soldiers into the harbor. They felt that this would be an ample show of force that would have Khalid back down from his claim to the throne. Much to the chagrin of the British troops, Khalid refused to back down stood his ground and quickly aimed his artillery at the British forces.

It didn't take long for the new Sultan to realize he was outgunned and outmanned, and so, early on the morning of August 27th, he sent a message to the British troops asking for a meeting. Knowing that they had the upper hand, the British said they would only agree to a conversation if all the terms that they set forth were agreed upon. Khalid sent a message back saying that he was optimistic that the British would never open fire on the palace, but he was proven wrong just an hour later.

While the palace was being attacked, the Royal Navy also attacked Zanzibar's navy, sinking one of their ships. It wasn't long before the British ceased fire, and the wannabe

Sultan surrendered. Five hundred of Khalid's men were either wounded or killed, and only one British soldier was injured.

Khalid fled to the German consulate where he found help to exit Zanzibar, after realizing he could not stay in his country.

That same afternoon, the British placed the person they had intended to put on the throne on the throne, and the shortest war in the world came to an end, having lasted just thirty-eight minutes.

Einstein For President!

At the end of WWII, the Allied Forces felt there was a need to proclaim a state for the Jews who were persecuted by many nations. And so, in 1948, then Jewish agency chairman, David Ben-Gurion, proclaimed Israel a state. He would later go on to become the first Prime Minister of Israel.

Chain Weizmann, who would take the seat of the first president of Israel and Ben-Gurion, would be put into power in 1949. However, only three years after he came into power, President Weizmann would pass away, leaving the newly founded Israeli government in need of a leader. But who would it be? In the end, Ben-Gurion felt he found the perfect person for the job. The Prime Minister decided that the famous scientist Albert Einstein, seventy-three at the time and not an Israeli citizen, would be the best choice.

With the decision made, the Prime Minister partnered with Abba Eban, the Israeli ambassador in Washington, to write a letter formally offering the job to Einstein—as long as the Knesset said it was okay. Once the letter was completed, it was sent via courier to Einstein. The letter offered citizenship to Einstein and said that the Israeli people and the government would support him fully in whatever endeavors he took as president. The Prime Minister went on to shower Einstein with praise and detail how his presidency of the newly-formed country would be a symbolic representation of the perseverance of the Jewish people and traditions.

Einstein heard the offer was on its way to him. He mulled the idea over and had already concluded what his answer would be well before he read the words of the Prime Minister.

Though he was honored, he declined the offer. He then phoned Eban to let him know his decision. Disappointed, the ambassador asked if the illustrious scientist would write a formal letter declining the offer. Einstein agreed and, sitting down at the desk, wrote a letter describing how he felt that he lacked the natural skills and ability to deal with people, especially in an official capacity.

History could have been very different, if only Einstein had taken the offer and become the second president of the Israeli state.

Who's Your Daddy?

In 1922, Howard Carter, a British archaeologist, would make the finding of a lifetime. As he was digging in the Valley of the Kings, he came across an unopened tomb that housed within it a plethora of artifacts including one sarcophagus that would become the most famous finds in the world. This archaeological find was that of the tomb of Tutankhamun.

When Tutankhamun's mummy was found, the world was obsessed with the young pharaoh. Who was this boy? When did he reign? And how did he die? As science continued to evolve, so did the tools and testing but it would take decades for these questions to be answered.

When the archaeologists got these tests back, it became clear who King Tut's grandfather and father were. His grandfather was one of the greatest pharaohs in history,

Amenhotep III, making his father the controversial Pharaoh Akhenaten. The Pharaoh Akhenaten tried to move Egypt's new Kingdom from the old religion to a religion that worshiped one sun god, Aten. On top of this, he also moved the capital from Thebes to Amarna. When Akhenaten died, the people, in some ways, rejoiced and returned to their old methods of worship. Once Tutankhamun took the throne, he changed everything back and began his rule. Even though we know his patrilineal line, the question of who Tutankhamun's mother still remained.

In 2010, after many DNA tests had been run, the results were published, and papers written that stated that Tutankhamun's parents were siblings; King Tut's mother may have been a daughter of Amenhotep III and, therefore, Akhenaten's sister. This familial relationship was why child sarcophaguses were found stashed inside with him when Tutankhamun's tomb was discovered. But this wasn't the only incestuous relationship. Some scholars speculated that King Tut's mother was actually Queen Nefertiti, making the boy king a product of familial incest because Nefertiti was Akhenaten's cousin.

Because of all the familial relationships, the answer to who exactly Tutankhamun's parents are may never be known. Still, one thing is for sure, they were definitely a close-knit family.

And The Award Goes To...

The Nobel Peace Prize is one of the most prestigious awards ever given to anyone. Starting in 1901, a committee based out of Norway was formed to determine who amongst the world leaders in several different categories showed the most zeal for reviving the idea of peace in their own nation or the globe.

These people can be nominated by anyone; which means sometimes nominees find their way on the list that might be pretty surprising to those in the outside world. Three of these illustrious nominees just so happened to be three of the world's most famous dictators. That's right, as you scroll down the list of past nominees, you're going to run across three very familiar names—Adolf Hitler, Joseph Stalin, and Benito Mussolini.

Due to the open nomination principle of this committee, Benito Mussolini was nominated in 1935 by two separate professors. Though there are no documents to support this claim, his name does appear on the list, and due to his less than savory treatment of political opposition and his dictatorship of terror, it is clear why he did not receive the award. But even still, the fact that he was nominated may sound pretty strange to many people—no stranger though than looking down the list and seeing Joseph Stalin.

Stalin, too, was a dictator who would go on to commit atrocities. His nominations (in 1945 and 1948) are actually understandable when looking at them through the lens of world history. Stalin played a significant role in ending WWII and with this, some say did play a role in bringing about peace.

Speaking of WWII, the last name that might surprise you on this list is Adolf Hitler. This nomination was not because the person thought that Hitler was actually someone who was looking to create a world of peace, it was of more an ironic joke. His nomination was in response to the Prime Minister of the United Kingdom being nominated. The nominator felt that Chamberlain's appointment was a farce because he had been just as culpable when it came to the strained relations between Germany, France, and the UK.

This story may sound weird and made up, but at least none of them went on to win.

Where Are You From?

There are a few names from Egyptian history that would be familiar to just about anyone, regardless of historical interest and expertise. Names like Tutankhamun and Nefertiti are among those, but maybe the most famous Egyptian ruler of all was Cleopatra VII. This Egyptian queen ruled her empire for several decades.

Known for her intellect and beauty, Cleopatra even found her way into the hearts of two of the most powerful men in the world, Julius Caesar and Marc Anthony. Because of her place in Egyptian history, many people assume that she was of Egyptian blood. Weirdly enough, that was not the case at all.

Cleopatra was born into the House of Ptolemy to Ptolemy XII Auletes and Cleopatra V, then the rulers of

Egypt. Like many of the royal houses, this couple were actually related and may well have been brother and sister. This illustrious queen, though allegedly a product of incest, didn't let this stop her from building her family dynasty to the next level. After all, the Ptolemaic dynasty had been ruling Egypt since 323 BC when Ptolemy I, a Macedonian general under Alexander the Great's rule, was handed the reins of Egypt.

This placement began the Egyptian period of Greek-speaking Pharaohs that lasted for three centuries. Though Cleopatra was fully aware that she was not of Egyptian descent, she had a deep love for the culture and embraced it with everything she had. Cleopatra even went so far as to be the first of her line to actually take the time to learn the Egyptian language, which helped her gain more support from the Egyptian people.

Torches Of Freedom

A lot was changing in the world in the early 1900s. With the First World War happening in this century, these changes included gender roles in the United States. Now, women were in the workforce and companies realized that they had to corner that market as well.

One of these industries that focused on the female market was tobacco. It was perfectly acceptable for men to smoke back then, but a woman smoking was seen as immoral. Old-fashioned ideas could actually land the woman in jail. As women became more and more willing to fight for equal rights, tobacco executives thought they could use this as a promotional tool to build sales in the female market.

George Washington Hill, who was then in charge of lucky strike cigarettes, hired a public relations guru to help him figure out how to tie in cigarette smoking with the feminist movement for equality.

The man who was charged with this had quite a hill in front of him, and his name was Edward Bernays. Of all the hurdles he had to leap, the highest one was trying to figure out how to take the social stigma of a female smoking in public and get rid of it. Looking to steer the narrative, Hill and Bernays also wanted to make smoking look feminine, and these two tasks would seemingly go hand in hand.

To reach their goal, they decided they had to hire a large group of women for the project. They knew they had to be careful with the selection because they didn't want anybody that seemed too beautiful nor too characterless. They needed these women to look like everyday women in order to drive the new PR campaign they were looking to use. This PR campaign became known as Torches of Freedom. They launched this PR campaign at one of the biggest parades of the time, the Easter parade. So on March 31, 1929, one of the women that they had hired, Bertha Hunt, walked out into the middle of 5th Avenue and lit a Lucky Strike cigarette.

The media was there to catch the scene as they had been told of this controversial act beforehand. With pride in his heart, Bernay's knowing that his campaign was already in motion and beginning to work, said that smoking was for female freedom and that every woman should jump on the bandwagon. It wasn't long before more young women took up the march behind Bertha hunt that day on 5th Avenue and lit cigarettes up just like she did.

Over the next six years, Lucky Strike doubled their sales because of this promotional campaign. Though the men behind the campaign had no desire to fight for equal rights for women, they were willing to market their product as a way for women to fight for their rights.

It seems very weird that there was a march for their right to smoke in public that became a legendary PR campaign for Lucky Strike cigarettes that masqueraded as a way to fight for women's rights.

That's One For The History Books

Many people across the globe look to have their name included in the annals of history by holding a world record. But in 2018, one history professor from the University of North Texas chose a unique way to get his name in the famous Guinness World Records book

Andrew Torget was a humanities teacher at the college and loved to give professional development workshops. Combining his love for history and his love for workshops, Andrew decided he would try for the world record when it came to the world's longest history lesson.

After weeks of preparing his lecture, the professor ended up with a history lesson that was set to run for twenty-six hours and thirty-three minutes. This lesson would cover the entire history of Texas from the prehistoric era all the way to the 20th century.

On August 24, at nine in the morning, with a PowerPoint presentation made of sixteen hundred slides and a binder full of five hundred pages of notes, he began his lecture. To capture this record, at least ten of the students had to remain awake for the entire lesson; otherwise, the professor would not capture that renowned title of the world's longest history lesson.

He was able to complete his lesson and meet all the requirements and gained his very own entry in the Guinness World Records book.

Anubis No, We Won't Go!

Strikes are not new, though many may think they started when unions became a tool to ensure workers were getting what they deserved. Strikes have been going on for centuries, and one of the first recorded actually happened all the way back during the rule of Pharaoh Ramses III.

Ramses had been having quite a bit of trouble with other empires, but he had managed to keep his people and his kingdom safe. To celebrate, and as he got closer to the thirtieth year of his rule, his officials decided to throw him a big party. However, three years before the festival in 1159 BCE, some issues began to arise. As all Pharaohs did, his tomb builders and artisans were hard at work in the process of building a mighty tomb. But when it came time for payment, there was no coin to be had. Their pay did eventually show up, but it was a month late. To keep the workers happy, one of Ramses' administrators distributed different grains.

Unfortunately for these administrators, this issue continued to pile up, and as time went by, the payment was becoming later and later. Frustrated with this situation, the necropolis workers couldn't take it any longer, and so they set their tools down and began to march into the city. They started at the Mortuary temple and then found their way to the temple of Thutmose III, where they staged what modern protesters would now call a sit-in.

Ramses' officials were perplexed; they had no idea what to do with this, and seeing as how the workers kept talking about being hungry, they thought a great way to assuage the issues of these workers was to feed them. In an effort to calm the problems, they had pastries sent to the workers. This act only served to agitate the workers more, and eventually, they stood up from their sit-in and marched on the central storehouse of Thebes. This maneuver was just the tactic they needed, and soon Ramses' officials found a way to get the payments to the workers. But it didn't take long for them to find out that the next payment was not available and was not intended to be delivered anytime soon.

Frustrated, the workers once again laid down their tools and went on strike. With the impending jubilee at hand, they decided the best option would be to set up camp at the opening of the Valley of the Kings. Not wanting to be disrespectful to their pharaoh, the jubilee did go on to much success. The strikes and issues with the worker's payment continued well after the festivities.

The Pharaoh's officials eventually corrected the problem but not before they went down in history as the very first strikes ever to be held.

Tom Dooley, Who?

In 1958, one of the hottest songs on the charts was a ballad by The Kingston Trio entitled, *Tom Dooley*, but this wasn't the first recording of this famous murder ballad.

Franken and Warner recorded a man singing the song in 1938. The song would go on to be recorded several other times, but who exactly was Tom Dooley and why was this song so popular remained a mystery. The piece starts with the hanging of Tom Dooley and tells the story of how he found himself on the gallows. Like many songs of this nature, it was based on a real-life event.

Tom Dula was sentenced to death by hanging in 1868, after being convicted of killing his one true love, Laura Foster, just two years prior. Plenty of mystery and intrigue surrounded the crime, and for generations, this tragic love story smeared with betrayal was passed down.

The story started in the 1860s, when the U.S. was thrown into an internal civil war between the North and the South. Before joining the military, Tom Dula was engaged and in love with a woman named Ann Melton. When the war ended, and Tom returned home, he found Ann was already married to someone else. Heartbroken, he realized this meant he had to move on, and he did with Ann's cousin, Laura Foster.

Just a few months later, Laura was found dead and buried in a shallow grave. It seems that she had been stabbed in the chest and the first suspect was her lover, Tom.

Tom was soon arrested and brought back to North Carolina to stand trial for her murder. The trial had many ups and downs, but Tom continued to claim his innocence.

Most people who passed the story along believed that Tom was actually innocent of the crime and that his jilted past lover, Ann Melton, had been the actual perpetrator.

Though some may think a story of this dubious nature inspiring a chart topping song is a little odd, it is not alone in its place in music history. Songs like *Mack the Knife* and *The*

Ballad of Tom Dooley are more common than you might think!

Hole Into Hell

An experimental well was drilled in the Kola Peninsula in 1984, back when it still was the Soviet Union. A group of geologists worked tirelessly in one of the remote parts of Siberia, drilling a hole that ended up being about nine miles deep. This simple geologic project would become the source of one of the biggest internet legends during the 1990s.

Though many scientists debunked the tale, some people still gravitate to believing that truth is much weirder than being told to the public. As the drill reached the nine-mile marker, the story goes, the bit began to rotate quite radically. The project manager, only known as Mr. Azzacov, and the team of geologists allegedly began to see the temperature gauge raise on their instruments up to over two thousand degrees Fahrenheit.

Feeling and registering this temperature, the team acted quickly and began to drop high-quality and sensitive microphones into the hole itself. As the mic dropped deeper and deeper, the team began to hear strange sounds. Eventually, as they neared the bottom, the noises became more audible and sounded like people screaming. The team then began to think they had drilled into the earth's center and found their way to hell.

The story has many different endings, two of the most popular endings being that the group either ran away from the site or was brave enough to confront these tortured souls.

Eventually, even with the taped recordings of the screaming souls from hell, the story was proven to be a hoax, but not before it found its way into media outlets and television broadcasts.

How people could be so gullible is a mystery in and of itself. Eventually, as the internet began to grow, the "Well to Hell" story grew and became one of those illustrious urban legends.

What's Eating You?

History is rife with stories of unspeakable acts and heinous crimes. So much so, that there seems to be an almost obsession with the perpetrators of these crimes. Who these criminals are and why they would do something so inhumane feeds this obsession. Sometimes the stories that come with these acts seem stranger than fiction. Take, for instance, the case of the celebrity criminal, Issei Sagawa.

In the summer of 1981, a couple watched a short Japanese man with two suitcases enter the Bois de Boulogne Park. The couple thought there was something odd about this young man, and they would eventually find the two suitcases he had brought into the park stashed under a hedge.

As they opened it, they would find the torso and dismembered body of what appeared to be a young woman.

They immediately called the police, and it didn't take long for law enforcement to arrive at the park. After investigating the crime scene and evaluating all the clues, the police quickly arrested the culprit.

The murderer was Issei Sagawa, who turned out to be a classmate of the now identified exchange student, Renee Hartevelt. The minute the officer sat down to interrogate the young man, he immediately confessed to killing Renee. He went on in some detail, telling the police that he had done so in the hopes that he could eat her. With this confession and the eyewitness testimony, this case should have been an open and shut one.

However, other evidence showed that the perpetrator wasn't sane enough to stand trial. Because of this, Sagawa was unable to be convicted of the crime and was sent back to his home country of Japan, where he was placed in a psychiatric hospital.

Japan then took up the mantle and tried to convict him, but eventually, this ended up backfiring, and Sagawa was released. He would later check himself into an institution of his own free will.

Like so many vicious criminals, Sagawa took the opportunity to utilize his infamy to make a little money instead of disappearing from the public eye. He authored several books and was also the subject of a few films and songs.

The fact that this man heinously murdered a young woman and never paid for his crime is tragic and hard to believe.

Migrating North

In the 70s, there was a lot of craziness happening around the world, from the Vietnam War to gas shortages and all other kinds of upheaval. Maybe one of the most well-known topics was that of the killer bees.

Headlines were splashed all over newspapers, and segments on local news discussed the impending invasion in detail, discussing the hybridization of the bees and how they were on their way to invade the United States. Playgrounds and households were in an uproar discussing how they could prevent being swarmed by these vicious bees when they arrived. The truth was there were African bees that had been brought to South America in the 1950s for a hybridization program. The aim of the program was to create a new species of bees that yielded more honey. Unfortunately, the breeding of these two bees heralded something completely different; producing instead bees that were more aggressive.

Through a series of unfortunate events, these bees escaped into the wild, and the story began to spread that they were migrating north towards the United States. However, the stories of these bees being deadly were blown out of proportion. In fact, there were only two differences between a regular honeybee and the Africanized bees. First, that the Africanized were more aggressive and second, that instead of a limited number swarming a threat, the whole hive would swarm.

As the panic began to grow, more and more news outlets started to use infographics to show the migration of these bees through Mexico and into the United States. Eventually, these bees did make it to the U.S., and though they were more aggressive than the ordinary honeybee, there was no call for widespread panic and fear for lives—unless you were allergic to bees. Upon arrival, these bees began to mate with the native honeybees of the southern United States and eventually became a more tame version of an Africanized bee.

The media circus surrounding the killer bees coming from South America to the U.S. was potential fodder for Hollywood. Taking a cue from the fear that this potential invasion had stoked, there were some movies made and several sketches on the popular Saturday night sketch show, Saturday Night Live.

Though the story was exaggerated, these little bees found their way into pop culture and are still being talked about to this very day.

Man Of Steel's Death

Hollywood may well be one of the most superstitious places in the world. With rumors of cursed scripts and cursed stages, there were many tales that seemed weird and made up. One of the most famous curses is called the Superman curse.

The Superman curse is centered around the unfortunate experiences of anyone that works on Superman-related properties. The alleged beginnings of this curse was with the Superman of the 50s, George Reeves. George Reeves played Superman from 1951 to 1958, in both the movies and in television. When the television series was over, this actor had difficulty finding a role in anything else. A year later, just days before he was set to be married to his current paramour Lenore Lemmon, George Reeves was shot dead in his home, where his body was also found.

Early on June 16, 1959, a gunshot was heard from the upstairs bedroom of Reeves. Those that were downstairs having drinks after a long night sat in shock after hearing the loud bang from upstairs. Details of what happened that night vary depending on who you talk to, but this may be because most of the four or five people downstairs, including Reeves' fiancé, were having drinks when they heard the noise.

George had retired upstairs earlier than the rest because he was irritated with the party downstairs and depressed because of his career's sudden downturn. When the party heard the gunshot from upstairs, they ran to the room where they found Reeves dead with a bullet hole and a gun lying next to him. The mystery starts here because the party took their time before calling the police. The men and women that had been in the house explained this away as shock and over-intoxication. So, in the end, Reeves death was ruled a suicide.

Though Reeves had been very depressed as of late, his mother could not take the ruling of a suicide as the final word. This disbelief could well have been because there were certain strange things about the case in general. When the police were doing their investigation, they found three shots in the room. There were two that hit the floor and one that hit Reeves. Aside from this, there were also reported comments made by his fiancé that seemed to allude to the fact she thought he would shoot himself. There were also no fingerprints found on the gun, and there was no gun residue test ever done on Reeves.

The private investigator that Reeves' mother hired stated that he felt the determination of the police was correct, and Reeves had actually committed suicide. But even with the police dictating that this was the result they came to after all the evidence was looked at, there are still rumors and theories that Reeves was actually killed.

With so much time having passed since the tragedy, the truth may never be known!

Foreign Origins

Nowadays, it's not surprising for anyone to find out that one of their favorite sitcoms or television shows in the U.S. actually started as a British show. This type of thing happens all the time now, but this was not the case in the 60s and 70s. Before, the fans and audiences thought that these shows were originals, yet they were actually borrowing quite a bit from across the pond. One of these that may be very shocking to most that is based on a British show is the hit sitcom, *All In The Family*.

From 1965 to 1975, a British sitcom called *Till Death Us Do Part* was just as controversial as its American version. The main character of that sitcom Alf Garnett was a significant factor in developing the iconic role portrayed by Carol O'Connor, Archie Bunker. The British Archie Bunker,

Alf Garnett, was like the American version—quick to insult and very opinionated, especially about politics and other social aspects of his life.

When Norman Lear, the creator of the American sitcom, was asked, he openly acknowledged the fact that Archie bunker was based on Garnett. However, he quickly added that there was a little bit of his dad thrown in, which is why the character has become so iconic and is well remembered to this very day.

A Town On Fire

Hollywood gets inspiration, especially in horror films and video games, from many real-life events and places. Silent Hill is one of the most famous video games, which later became a series of very popular horror films. It is based on a small town in Pennsylvania called Centralia, which now sits abandoned, with smoke of the perpetual fires still swirling through the air.

At one point, Centralia was a bustling mining town, but in 1962, a spark would ignite a fire that would leave this town burning for decades to come.

By the 1950s and 60s, Centralia had developed many issues that were not being properly taken care of by city officials. One of these issues was the garbage from both the businesses and the residents, which tended to be tossed into the Centralia landfill. This abandoned mine had become a garbage dump, but it wasn't the only unregulated dump throughout the city. This situation left the city with a distinct odor and a rodent problem.

In May of 1962, tired of the issues with the landfill, the city council proposed a cleanup process so that they would be ready to celebrate Memorial Day properly. But the method they chose to do this turned out to be a fatal mistake. They opted to burn the trash, and unfortunately, a spark from this fire found its way into a crack and into the mines underneath the town.

It didn't take long for this fire to expand throughout the tunnels underneath the city and the smoke began billowing from cracks in the ground. As the fire became larger and larger, many local mines started to close down due to too much carbon monoxide in the tunnels. They tried to excavate and put the fire out to save their town, but none of these excavations were successful. As the years went by, the ground itself began to radiate temperatures that were unlivable for people.

In fact, some of these temperatures reached insane numbers as high as nine hundred degrees Fahrenheit. Smoke began to billow, and sinkholes even began to form. Eventually, the residents began experiencing health issues caused by the fire and had to find a way out of the town.

In 1992, the federal government stepped in and bought out anybody living in Centralia and condemned the buildings. The city is now abandoned and still burns to this day.

Elvis & The FBI

Elvis Presley has been the subject of different strange theories and urban legends. Many people believe that he actually did not die, but was taken into FBI protective custody due to his relationship with this government agency. But the story of how Elvis got involved with the FBI is an even stranger tale.

In December of 1970, the secret service at the entry to the White House were shocked to look up and see Elvis Presley standing in front of them. In his hand was a letter addressed to President Richard Nixon that he wanted delivered that day.

Two days earlier, Elvis had had a major fight with his then-wife Priscilla and had gone to the airport and hopped on the first flight out. This flight just so happened to be heading to Washington, DC. Though initially, he didn't stay and instead opted to go to LA. Once he arrived in LA, for some reason, he turned around and flew back to Washington D.C.. Elvis shared the flight with a senator who struck a conversation with him and later on urged him to write a letter to President Nixon, asking for a meeting.

The next day, Elvis left the letter with the White House staff at the gate, and the heartfelt note found its way into the president's hands. As Nixon read through the letter, he was taken by Elvis's passion for wanting to help his country, until he got to an extraordinary passage where Elvis expressed that he wanted something in return for his help. It seemed Elvis Presley decided that he wanted to be a federal agent to help curb the growing drug problem in America.

Nixon, taken for some reason by the words of Elvis, agreed to the meeting. When the meeting took place, Elvis, like any good guest, showed up with a present for the president. He also showed Nixon his prized collection of police badges from various places across the country.

After the niceties had been exchanged, Elvis reiterated his desire to be granted a Narcotics Bureau badge and the title of FBI agent. After a bit of deliberation with some of his advisers, Nixon agreed that he would give Elvis an honorary agent at large title. With a handshake and embrace, the two parted ways, with Elvis ensuring Nixon that he would do a good job.

This story would have never been told if not for a Washington Post journalist and their exposé on the meeting that ran in the January 27, 1972 newspaper.

Smile, You're Being Murdered

The internet birthed many urban legends, and several of those have some root in the truth. Some of these have even been used as Hollywood movie plots; like the *Slender Man* or the *Smiley Face Murders* have grabbed the attention and imagination of countless people across the globe. But are the stories true or just overactive imagination run wild? It's a lot easier to believe in them when law enforcement professionals are referring to them left and right, as is the case with the infamous *Smiley Face Murders*.

In 1997, a college student, Patrick McNeil, was found drowned in New York City. Ruled as an accident due to alcohol intoxication, it seemed as if this case would be closed quickly. But for detectives Kevin Gannon and Anthony Duarte, there was just something that didn't seem quite right.

The young man's parents' impassioned pleas for further investigation gave these two detectives the courage to continue investigating this case long after it was closed.

Both of the detectives eventually retired but they continued their investigations which included tracking a series of drowning deaths of young men that occurred along the I-94 corridor from Michigan to Montana. It didn't take long for this duo to become a four-person team, as Gannon and Duarte were joined by two other detectives. tThe team dug further and further into these closed cases, eventually coming up with the idea that these were actually homicides conducted by an organized group of serial killers, working together to evade the authorities. At over a dozen of these deaths, investigators noted that there was graffiti of a smiley face nearby—they began calling this organized group of killers the *Smiley Face killers*.

This theory and the team that founded it began to gain national media attention, spurring on many other investigations into the *Smiley Face Killers*. Many of these investigations asked questions about the inconclusive information and the details provided by the team. Because of this, there were several research studies done by places like the Center for Homicide Research and the FBI on the cases.

However, there was no convincing evidence, and most law enforcement agencies believe the *Smiley Face Killers* theory to be nothing more than a hoax.

Play Me A Little Song

The streets of New Orleans in 1918 were filled with fear and uncertainty due to a series of violent murders. With over twelve people attacked during his reign over the city that lasted for nearly a year, this serial killer became a legend among the quarters of New Orleans. The murders were being executed by a man whose primary weapon of choice was the axe which earned him the name the *Axeman of New Orleans*.

The *Axeman*'s first two attacks were deemed coincidences, but as the police began investigating the third attack, it soon became evident that these murders were connected. Not only had the killer targeted the Italian community, but it seemed that he preferred homes that had axes. Though not all the murders fit this modus operandi, it was as if this serial killer was taking out his anger in the homes of New Orleans.

With the murders gaining more media coverage, everybody in New Orleans's Italian community was on edge. Vigilante neighborhood watch groups were beginning to prowl the streets at night and report suspicious men and axes throughout the city. Because of the combined vigilance of the people and the police, it seemed the *Axeman* had ended his reign of terror.

Then ten months after the attack on Sarah Lawman, the *Axeman* once again reared his head. With three more attacks under his belt, it seemed like the *Axeman* was back in his groove and on the prowl. Then something strange occurred. The *Axeman* decided he wanted to make a splash in the papers and wrote a letter that would cement his place in history.

In this letter, he claimed to be a spirit passing over the city of New Orleans. Even more cryptically, he wrote that his next attacks would happen on the coming Tuesday, unless the people of New Orleans played jazz from every home and every establishment in the city. This declaration caused a panic, and the people began to purchase record players and jazz records by the dozens. As the hour approached that evening, jazz drifted through the air, and true to his word, there were no attacks that evening.

The *Axeman of New Orleans* would never attack again. Since those fearful months in 1919, there have been many theories about who this serial killer was, but none have been proven. To this day, his identity remains a mystery.

Brushy Bill

The old west was full of lawmen and outlaws if the tales are to be believed. Many legends about lawmen like Wyatt Earp and outlaws like Billy the Kid have stood the test of time and are still told to this very day.

Billy the Kid went by many different names and began his criminal career at the age of sixteen. By the time he was eighteen, he had already killed someone, and by the age of twenty-one, his legend would come to a fatal end. Shot by Sheriff Pat Garrett in a shootout near Fort Sumner, New Mexico, the young, charismatic, old west outlaw would die before his life had even really begun. That is, if you believe that he was actually killed in that shootout.

Some believe that Billy made it out of the shootout alive and that Pat Garrett helped cover this up, so that Billy could start life anew. Others believe that Pat Garrett, who allegedly killed Billy in a shootout, was shooting in the dark and accidentally hit the wrong man. Not willing to admit that he had missed the mark, the sheriff proclaimed it was Billy and quickly buried him in the cemetery.

Visitors of the Billy the Kid Museum will see some speculations that Billy moved to Texas in 1883, and took on the name of William Henry Roberts. This date would have been two years after his supposed death. William Henry was more lovingly known to the folks of Hico, Texas, as "Brushy" Bill Roberts. How did the museum come upon this idea? Not long after Billy was buried, one of his associates hired a probate investigator named William Morrison to ensure that Billy had really died.

While the probate investigator was on his mission, he seemed to come upon some evidence. He told his client that Billy was actually still alive and had built a life for himself in Texas. Interested in the fact that Billy the Kid might still be alive, the probate investigator took a little trip out to Texas to meet the alleged Billy the Kid. During this meeting, Brushy Bill admitted to being Billy the Kid and pled with the probate investigator to help him prove it so that he could get a pardon for his crimes. After all, the governor in Mexico had promised him one back in the 1800s, and Brushy Bill just wanted to clear his name.

Unfortunately, there was no proof that this gentleman who claimed to be with Billy Kid was actually the outlaw himself. Because of this, he never received the pardon, and his identity was a subject of debate for historians in the United States for decades to come.

Lake Monsters In North America

One of the biggest mysteries that has stood the test of time is that interesting lake monster from Scotland. The Loch Ness Monster certainly has captured the attention and imagination of many generations, but it is not the only lake monster in the world. Many might be surprised to know that several different types of lake monsters can be found in the lakes of North America.

The legend of Champy, which resides in Lake Champlain, is one of the most well-known tales, but there are also monsters and lesser-known parts of the Americas. What they are and why they inhabit these lakes is a mystery.

Take for instance, the half-man, half-goat animal that was said to dwell in Lake Worth Perry, just outside Fort Worth, TX. In 1969, the people from this small town panicked when sightings of the weird animal around the lake were reported. The story goes that this creature would come to the surface and hop on land to terrorize the people around the lake. After the hysteria had calmed down, the reports of the creature also began to diminish. This tale is still told, with many theories surrounding what the beast was, including one involving a gorilla costume.

Yet another strange North American lake monster dwells in Herrington Lake, Kentucky. This lake monster was described as an eel with a pig-shaped head and a curly tail. Those Kentuckians that had witnessed this lake monster said that it was about fifteen feet long and super-fast. This seems to be a common theme among many other North American sea monsters; of which there are many more than just these two.

There are several different theories. For this one, there was talk of a creature that descended from the dinosaurs or giant alligators. No matter which lake monster tale, the monster is often described made up of many animals and that makes for some weird stories.

One More Time

Literary figures throughout the ages have had exciting lives and deaths that would go on to be discussed for centuries to come. In the 19th and 20th century, one of these interesting literary figures was definitely Ambrose Bierce.

This brilliant albeit morbid and a little bitter author would author stories that told the tale of the period with eloquence. He would write in-depth descriptions of the Civil War and delve into the supernatural adventures that were so popular at the time. Ambrose was able to use language like few others could and make the reader elicit very powerful feelings.

Ambrose was one of those literary figures that, due to his body of work and talent, has inspired historians to study his life. Even though there is so much written about him there is still one thing that remains a mystery—his death.

After years of delivering tales and stories that captivated his readers, Ambrose decided to leave the United States and head for Mexico. He had outlived his two children and been separated from his wife for years. These life occurrences left him bitter and alone. Ambrose wanted to visit the places that were potentially filled with exciting events and were different than what he was used to. His letters to friends back home detailed his itinerary, starting from Mexico to South America and across the Andes. He chose Mexico, a place where revolution was brewing, as his first destination.

In October of 1913, the writer took off for Mexico after a year of intense travel through old battlefields from the Civil War. When diving into the mystery surrounding this author's death, many people have concluded that Ambrose himself felt this would be his final trip and would not return from Mexico.

Ambrose started his trip by crossing the border near El Paso and entering the small Mexican city of Juarez. He was immediately greeted by Poncho Villa and his soldiers. Joining Poncho Villa's army and riding with him, Bierce would venture South. His last letter would be sent December 26, 1913, and this was the last time anyone heard from Ambrose Bierce.

What happened to the author is unknown, and this mystery has led to multiple theories of how the author met his end. Some think he died riding alongside Poncho Villa, while others say that he simply passed away from the stress and anxiety of being involved with the battle.

Dance Until You Die!

In the Middle Ages, medicine and science had limited answers to many of the epidemics that plagued the countries and empires of the time. Most of these epidemics were common illnesses that would leave people laid up in bed with excruciating and horrible symptoms. However, not all of the epidemics would manifest like this.

One of the weirdest epidemics happened in July 1518, when the city of Strasbourg was suddenly struck by an overwhelming desire to get out on the dance floor. The epidemic started with one woman, Frau Troffea, who suddenly began to dance and twirl for no reason in the middle of the street. This woman continued to dance on her own for almost a week. More people began to have the same reaction during this time, and soon over three dozen people had shown signs of this affliction.

One month later, this epidemic had taken four hundred lives. The local physicians could not answer what was causing this at first, but eventually, they would blame something they called hot blood. The only way to get rid of this was to get out there and dance until you could get rid of the fever. To help this, the local authorities and physicians built a stage where patients could dance even going so far as to hire professional dancers, who could dance with the patients and a professional band, who could play the music. Sadly, by the time the stage was built, many people had died from exhaustion, stroke, or heart attack.

After two months of this, with no end in sight, authorities decided it was time to go the more religious route. They took the dancers up into the mountains to a monastery so that they could pray for forgiveness.

What may have caused this epidemic of dance in Strasburg? In the 1500s, many people felt that this was a curse placed on them by Saint Vitus. With everything that the people were facing, such as other diseases and famine, the idea that a saint would curse anyone with the dancing plague may have caused hysteria. There were even theories that this plague was caused by a religious cult or ergot in the grain-a hallucinogen that can cause spasms and irregular behavior.

The tale of the dancing plague is definitely a weird story that most find hard to believe.

The Korean Invasion of 1871

If you ask people when was the first time the United States entered Korea, most everyone would say in the 1950s. This 50s conflict was known as the Korean War and was when the United States came to the aid of South Korea to stop the progress of the communist army from the north. However, this was not the first time that America had invaded Korea by any stretch of the imagination.

The first conflict actually started in the latter part of the 1800s. Like many of the world's other major powers, the United States, was looking to expand into Asia for political and economic reasons. In 1866, a merchant ship from the United States called the General Sherman, dropped anchor off the coast of Korea. However, the boat itself disappeared. Five years later, the United States sent their ambassador with

143

a small squadron to Korea to investigate the disappearance of this ship and discuss opening up trade relations with the Korean government.

The Korean government in power at that time wanted nothing to do with the United States. To show them this, the Korean coastal defenses began shooting at two warships that were floating down the Han river. In retaliation, the ambassador decided that U.S. forces would attack the forts until the Koreans gave up and apologized for their aggressive actions. However, this tactic did not work. The Korean officials sent letters to the Americans, explaining that U.S. forces broke the law, as well as detailing what happened to General Sherman, and one of the Korean governors also sent other trinkets to discourage the U.S. from attacking the forts.

The Americans rejected the blunt letter and the gifts from the Koreans and continued attacking. In June of 1871, more than six hundred American soldiers landed and took charge of several Korean forts along the riverbank, killing more than two hundred Korean troops.

This major tactical operation ended with the Koreans and the Americans staying in conflict for over a decade. In

1882, the dispute was finally resolved with the signing of the Joseon-United States Treaty.

Though the invasion itself was not altogether weird, it does seem a bit weird that this conflict has been lost to the annals of time and left out of history classes across the United States.

The Barefoot Bandit

In June of 2010, a wave of thefts would come to an end with the capture of the criminal known as the *Barefoot Bandit*. Colton Harris-Moore, who had over his lengthy criminal career earned the name, lived in Camano Island, Washington. By the time Colton was caught, authorities would connect over one hundred crimes to him, including bank robbery, theft of bicycles, cars, speed boats, and transportation of stolen aircraft, throughout Washington, Idaho, and Canada.

Colton had been a convicted criminal since the age of twelve and continued his criminal activity up until the age of nineteen, when he was caught. After evading authorities for so long, several strange events in 2010 all lined up, which eventually helped the police catch Colton.

The first strange occurrence was a letter signed by the *Barefoot Bandit* that arrived at an animal shelter. The young criminal left that letter with a hundred dollar haul from one of his robberies.

Late in the summer of 2010, the authorities were closing in and Colton decided it was time to make a run for it. After he crossed the state of Indiana by stealing different types of vehicles, he realized he needed to go a little bit further. He found a local airfield and jumped in a plane, quickly taking off before the owner could even notice that the plane was gone.

How the heck did this nineteen-year-old know how to fly? The authorities wondered the same thing but eventually concluded that he must have taught himself how to do it by looking up YouTube videos. Colton set off for the Bahamas, flying the plane with absolutely no training or hours in the air. Unfortunately, he wouldn't make it to the island. Colton lost control of his plane and had to crash land in the shallow waters surrounding one of the islands. He then set off on foot, trying to find another form of transportation, but regrettably, the FBI and the local police were able to capture him.

The barefoot bandit would eventually be sentenced in 2011 to seven years in prison. Colton would show genuine remorse and talk about his future, and in 2014, the young man was released from prison to try to build a life.

The crime spree had been perpetrated by someone that the world would never expect and filled with weird occurrences. From a letter with a small donation to an animal shelter to the fact that someone so young was able to steal things like planes, the story of the *Barefoot Bandit* was one strange tale.

Creepy Moths

There are some pretty interesting facts when it comes to animals and insects around the world. One example of these insects is a moth. There are many things that most people don't realize about these seemingly harmless insects. During the moth's life, they will go through four different stages before finally maturing.

The Luna moth is born without a mouth or a digestive system. This lack of a mouth means that they are only alive for a short amount of time, and during this time, their only goal is to mate. They can't eat when fully mature, so they eat a lot as caterpillar to stock up for the week-long life.

The Luna moth may be one of the most beautiful moths out there. They have lightly shaded green wings and a long tail. Once out of the cocoon, their wings span is about five inches, making them the largest moth in North America. These beautiful moths are nocturnal, and it takes seven days for their eggs to hatch.

Typically the Caterpillar phase ranges from three to four weeks, and often you can find these moths in trees like walnut or birch. Luna moths, though, are not the only moth species that mature without a mouth.

Other types of moths, like the Rosy Maple moth, build up their strength for their week-long expedition into the world, feeding off of maple and oak trees. Meanwhile, another kind of mouthless moth known as the Polyphemus, lives in forests and marshes scattered around from Canada all the way down to Mexico.

Aside from this species, two different kinds of mouthless moths called the Atlas moth, and the Prometheus moth can be found in other areas. The Atlas moth roams around South East Asia while the Prometheus moths live in the eastern and central United States.

The Unsinkable Kitty

For centuries, vessels that sail the open waters often kept at least one cat on board. These felines were primarily used to eliminate the rats and mice that found their way onto the ships. The presence of cats would keep the population of these rodents down, therefore protecting the provisions and equipment, while at the same time lessening the possibilities of disease spreading.

In WWII, one of these fortunate felines had quite a wartime career. Oscar started his naval career as part of the German naval fleet on a little vessel called the Bismarck. When Oscar and his crew left port in February 1939, they immediately saw combat in a battle against a British vessel called the Prince of Wales. During this battle, the Bismarck was damaged and eventually sank.

One hundred eighteen crewmen found their way to safety. Just a few hours after the vessel had sunk entirely, Oscar was also rescued while floating on a board. In fact, this fortunate feline was the only German naval survivor picked up by one of the allied vessels.

Taken in and considered a member of the crew on the HMS Cossack, he also received a new name, Unsinkable Sam. This cat had unknowingly switched sides and began his duties as part of the Royal Navy immediately. However, he wasn't to be on this boat for very long. The Cossack sailed to the Mediterranean and North Atlantic to escort convoys. All was well until an enemy torpedo damaged the vessel just a day after the German vessel was destroyed, the ship sank, and once again, Sam was now adrift on one of the remaining planks in the water.

Sam soon found a new home on the HMS Ark Royal after he was rescued by the crew.

This vessel had quite the reputation and was often called a lucky ship because it survived a handful of attacks. Unfortunately for this vessel, though, on November 14, it was torpedoed by a German submarine.

Once again, the poor feline was left to fend for its life floating on a plank through the waters. Tired of constantly being on the brink of death, the Royal Navy soon sent Sam to a land position in Gibraltar.

This very lucky cat spent his remaining time in the service there and eventually retired to Belfast, where he lived in a home for sailors until he passed away fourteen years after his first brush with death.

Hemingway's New Atlantis

Perhaps one of the most famous American authors is Ernest Hemingway, but he was not the only Hemingway who was a well-known author nor was he the only one who lived a fascinating life.

Ernest's younger brother, Leicester, was also an acclaimed author after having written six books, one of which is a WWII memoir titled, *My Brother, Ernest Hemmingway*. He also wrote *The Sound of the Trumpet*, which talked about young Hemingway's experiences during WWII.

Leicester was most remembered for founding a micronation he called "New Atlantis."

New Atlantis was established in 1965, and set up on a bank just six and a half miles off the coast of Jamaica;Hemingway was both the founder and president.

The island nation was crafted using a bamboo raft, iron pipe, steel cable, and stones. The tiny nation rose just fifty feet above the water and even had its own flag. The nation's flag was sewn by Leicester's wife, Doris. It was a navy blue flag with a golden triangle pointed downward, crafted out of the sailcloth they had lying around.

Many said that he was unable to do this, but he had the law on his side. In 1856, a federal law called the Guano Islands Act was enacted and it stated if there was sea bird or bat poop on any land formation, it could be claimed by the United States as long as it wasn't in international waters.

To make his claim legal, Hemingway made sure that the micronation was split in half, with part of it being in U.S. waters. Then he went and got himself some bat poop and made it legal.

The eccentric writer wasn't playing either, and to make people understand how legitimate his new micronation was, he also printed currency and stamps. He set up a post office box and sent letters to the United States president from New

Atlantis. Along with the letter to the then-president, he also gave the first lady and her daughters the coveted Order of the Golden Sand Honor.

In response to this letter and the kindness that young Hemingway had shown his family, President Johnson responded to the letter addressing the new leader of this micronation as president of New Atlantis. This acknowledgment gave him international recognition and made his claim more legitimate.

Swallow It Whole

Over the centuries, there have been some crazy trends out there. One of the craziest, started in the 1920s and carried on through the 1930s. During this period, tons of college students took the challenge to swallow live goldfish, which became quite the competition.

Though no one is sure exactly where this trend started, one popular theory, is that it was introduced by a student running for class president who had the campaign slogan: "Willing to do Anything."

Apparently, this meant swallowing a live goldfish, repeating this process in front of his peers over and over, and soon local media got hold of the story. It spread so quickly that Time Magazine did a piece on him. With so much attention placed on this young gentleman, suddenly everybody wanted to swallow live goldfish.

It eventually became a competition throughout the Ivy League colleges of the United States. The highest records of most live goldfish swallowed ranged from twenty-five all the way up to eighty-nine. The fad became very popular, and it also became apparent that the only way people would stop swallowing live goldfish was if the government intervened.

This political maneuver is precisely what happened when Massachusetts legislators opened up the session with a ban on the cruel consumption of live fish. Of course, this law was backed by local animal advocates, and it could lead to potential arrest for perpetrating this heinous act.

The United States government publicly chastised anyone taking part in this challenge. The government released a statement about how live fish could contain tapeworms and be unhealthy for the population to ingest.

These legislations negatively affected the reputation of several universities who sought ways to retaliate. Multiple universities published a study that said one hundred fifty live goldfish fish could be swallowed by an adult male and not have any adverse effects to their health. Thankfully, this research study didn't bring the craze back to the height of its popularity.

The practice never completely went away as it was alive and well all the way up into the 2000s, with many people posting videos and pictures of swallowing live goldfish despite the plethora of laws that were put in place against it.

Ronald Reagan's LP

Ronald Reagan started his career in Hollywood and, like many celebrities do nowadays, built a fanbase that would later launch him into political office. Born in 1911, Ronald Reagan became the governor of California from 1967 to 1975, and would eventually become the fortieth President of the United States in 1981. He would serve two presidential terms, during which several major world events occurred, including the fall of the Soviet Union and the destruction of the Berlin Wall.

Aside from being famous on television and on the silver screen, Reagan also gained fame as a recording artist. In fact, in 1961, he released a record titled, *Ronald Reagan Speaks Out Against Socialized Medicine*. This topic was already controversial, even back in the 60s and it was something that politicians on both sides felt the need to discuss regularly.

The record itself took on things like social security and warned Americans that their freedom would be restricted if the government went for a subsidized medical system. The album was released to mixed reviews depending, of course, on which side of the aisle you sat on. It was precisely how they felt for those in the Republican party and a response to many democratic bills that were being put to the vote in the hallowed halls of the American Congress and the Senate.

For the Democrats, it became fodder for Governor Pat Brown, who was running against Reagan in the 1966 gubernatorial race in California. Later, in 1980, when Jimmy Carter was going for reelection, the contents of the LP sparked controversy in the debate. Eventually, Reagan's view won out, and he became president of the United States.

It seems funny that this all started with the spoken word album by one of America's most beloved actors.

The Madness Of Nikola Tesla

During the early part of the 20th century, scientific advances were being discovered quite consistently. These scientific advances came from many names that are as famous now as they were then. One of those names was Nikola Tesla, a Serbian-American engineer and physicist, diving into everything having to do with electricity.

This genius was the first person to create an alternating current motor and was the primary rival of another famous scientist from this era, Thomas Edison. Though in the annals of history, Nikola Tesla doesn't get nearly as much credit for his discoveries as his rival, he was still one of the most influential scientists of the time. However, along with that genius, came a healthy dose of madness.

Nikola Tesla was perhaps the epitome of a mad scientist. He would produce bolts of lightning that were one hundred thirty-five feet long, and concentrate on strange inventions, like particle guns and different types of airplanes. He even worked on anti-gravitational flying machines and conducted extensive research into x-rays and electricity, which gained him popularity.

As time passed, this genius slowly became a slave to his obsessive-compulsive disorders. He would find himself having to do things in threes and being deathly afraid of touching human hair. Though this is strange, that is by far not the craziest thing that happened to him. Eventually, as his madness grew, he began raving about being in contact with extraterrestrials and even finding love... with a pigeon, who he claimed loved him back.

Nikola Tesla would continue his downward spiral. He would eventually pass away alone in a hotel room in New York City, leaving behind a debt of massive proportions.

After he passed, the FBI confiscated all his papers and research, deeming them top secret.

Fine Arts & The Olympics

Whether held in summer or in winter, the Olympic Games is one of the biggest sporting events. Originally held in Greece way back in 776 BC, these athletic games were forgotten for quite a while. But in 1896, the competition made a comeback. Through the decades after its reemergence, the events evolved creating a stark difference between the Olympics we know today and the one first held in 1896.

The International Olympic Committee (IOC) was created in 1894, and its initial task was to plan for the first few Olympic Games. With the first games in 1896, two hundred forty-one athletes from fourteen nations competed in forty-three different events. However one member of the

Olympic Committee, Baron Pierre de Coubertin, felt that something was missing.

Harkening back to the Greeks who inspired the events, Pierre de Coubertin felt the need for competitions that challenged both body and soul. This meant adding some fine arts competitions into the games. Beginning in 1906, the committee finally agreed to include five different events in this field. There were competitions in literature, music, sculpture, architecture, and painting.

The events under the fine arts category debuted during the London Games in 1908. Unfortunately, it was not as easy as athletic events to decide who would win the medals in an art competition. The difficulty persisted through each of the consecutive Olympic Games, and eventually, in 1948, fine arts at the Olympics would have its final run.

The arts would not be included in the Olympic Games for several decades, but in 2002 a form of the fine arts competition was added back into the Olympics.

The IOC decided it was essential to have an art contest, which include sculpting and graphic arts, but no medals were won, only cash rewards.

Can You Put A Little Medicine On My Burger?

Few people in the world could go without ketchup when eating food like hamburgers or French fries. This delicious, tomatoey treat has a unique origin story and may seem a little weird to people today.

One day in 1834, Dr. John Cook Bennett took a pre-existing concoction and threw in some tomatoes. Before the tomato was added, this concoction was called mushroom ketchup and was made with either a fish sauce or mushrooms. The doctor knew that by adding tomatoes, the sauce would be rich with vitamins and antioxidants. After he added the tomatoes, the doctor made wild claims that ketchup would be able to cure indigestion, rheumatism, diarrhea, and jaundice, to name a few afflictions.

166

Bennett later partnered with Archibald Miles, a pills salesman, and together they turned tomato ketchup into pills marketed as extracts of tomato. Then, Dr. Bennet released this new medicine out to the world.

When Bennett's tomato-based pills hit the market, many counterfeits and imitation tomato pills were released soon after, stirring many controversies. These controversies were caused by other doctors who created their own version of ketchup pills, filled with laxatives instead of tomatoes. These other doctors made impossible declarations claiming that their pills could cure terminal illnesses.

Because of this false advertisement, ketchup as a medicine soon fell out of favor just about two decades after being put on the market. That being said, people loved the flavor and would later use tomato ketchup as a condiment instead.

No Vodka!

After almost every significant event in a person's life, there comes a party. For some people, it doesn't matter how big or small the accomplishment is. There is always a reason to get some friends together and party the night away. Typically this means tons of food and a lot of liquor. Like any person, a country that has gone through years and years of devastation and destruction may need to celebrate and let off some steam. On May 9, 1945, this is just what Russia did.

With the final surrender of Germany, WWII came to a close. Some might assume that the Russian forces and people would wait to celebrate, but the party began when the Germans completed their surrender. The streets began to fill with people, and with those people came bottles of vodka.

Russia was in a bit of a vodka decline. Not only were their grain and starch sources drastically reduced, but the alcohol was also used as an antiseptic. Because of the importance of the clear liquid, Stalin himself had focused on production, but this created a severe shortage.

This raging party took what limited resources they had when it came to Vodka and depleted them to practically nothing, which is how Russia wound up a dry nation for a short period after the war.

Edison's Inadvertent Creation Of Hollywood

Every country has its motion picture capital. For the people of the United States, this motion picture capital is Hollywood in Los Angeles, California. There are many reasons why Hollywood was chosen: the weather was pretty consistent year-round, there were a lot of different types of scenery that could be used for shoots.

When the first studio was built in 1915, the land was affordable. But these were not the only reasons why the movie industry moved from the east coast to the west coast in the early part of the 1900s. One of the primary causes was the egotistical and somewhat dictatorial control of the New York movie industry by Thomas Edison.

Edison controlled over one thousand patents, and many of them were directly correlated to pieces of equipment needed for filmmaking: from the incandescent light bulb to the phonograph and the kinetoscope used in the earliest form of the movie camera.

His tight control on these patents and celebrity-status made it easy for him to convince other patent holders to work with him to form what would become known as the Motion Picture Patent Company (MPPC). This company allowed Edison and colleagues to monopolize every aspect of film.

The creation of this conglomerate meant if an individual wanted to be a filmmaker, they had to work with Edison. If someone dared to use a piece of equipment without their permission, Edison and the MPPC would take them to court. There were even rumors that if the individuals were unwilling to pay up, more extreme measures were taken, and some say this included working with the mob.

For those independent and determined filmmakers who wanted nothing to do with Edison, there was only one option: pack their equipment and their studios up and head west, where the patents that Edison held were not enforceable.

Not only were the courts not friendly to Edison, but it would be costly for him and the MPPC to try to take anyone to court when based on the opposite coast. On top of the good weather and the cheap land, Hollywood became the United States film mecca because of Edison and his tightfisted control on all his patents.

Do You Hear That?

Over the years, there have been many sayings that have come into use globally. Things like "in the nick of time" or "gone to pot" are expressions that most people have heard at least once. One of the most common sayings is "saved by the bell," which has multiple origin stories.

Some claimed that this expression was developed from boxing slang. In the 1800s , this phrase referred to the bell that would end the round during a boxing match. Typically when a boxer was about to lose the fight, and the bell would ring to end the round, it was as if that bell saved the boxer from being beat. Though that is a by far the least familiar origin story among the options.

The second story is probably the most popular when it comes to telling the tale of where the phrase came from.

During the 1600s, many plagues and pandemics were going around. Medicine was also not as well-trusted as it is today, and many people who were declared dead were buried when they weren't actually dead. Because this happened so frequently, many coffins were specifically designed to remedy the issue. Coffins were made with a hole in the top and the undertaker would wrap a string around one finger of the corpse and feed the string through the hole attaching it to a bell above ground. This way, if the person was not dead, they would wake up, ring the bell, and someone would come dig them up.

No matter which origin story a person prefers, both are pretty weird and very interesting.

You're Looking For The Other Paris

There are countless stories of brilliant military strategies that abound throughout history. Some of these are well celebrated, and others waited decades to come to light, like building a second Paris during WWI to confuse German bombers. This fake Paris even included Champs-Elysées and Gare du Nord.

The logic behind this tactic was the French military and government could build a life-like replica of Paris that the German pilots would assume was the real Paris. Therefore, the actual Paris would be saved from devastation and destruction. When the tactic was approved, French military planners set about building a life-sized replica just north of Paris.

Paris, even in the early 20th century, had already been dubbed the city of lights. Because of this, the military planners knew they had to include lights when drafting the plans for this replica. They hired an experienced and well-known electrical engineer to help design the plans to illuminate the streets with electric lights. When turned on in the evening, these lights would be a beacon drawing the German fighter pilots in and, therefore, would save the peak population and buildings of Paris from any potential danger.

To ensure that there was no question in the German bomber's minds whether this was Paris or not, the military architects also included several iconic landmarks like the train station, Arc de Triomphe, and the Paris Opera. They even went so far as to include industrial suburbs, which would have been the German bombers' primary target.

Once the skeletons of the buildings were laid out, the finishing touches were made. These included using translucent paint to make buildings look dirty and place flashing lights in the factories to look like machines were operating in there. The military planners even put in railroad tracks and fake trains to make everything look as realistic as possible. No one knows for sure if the plan actually worked because once the war was over, this fake Paris was quickly taken down and built over.

This fake city was forgotten until 2018, when a French newspaper journalist gearing up for the Armistice anniversary released an article about this military secret. It was only then that people learned about the second Paris.

Seeded From Above

Anyone who studied molecular biology or neuroscience will be familiar with the name Francis Crick. Crick and two other scientists played a significant role in understanding human DNA and its Helix structure. James Watson and Francis Crick attended the University of Cambridge and soon began working on their groundbreaking research.

In 1962, Watson and Crick won a Nobel Peace Prize in Physiology for their discovery of the molecular structure of nucleic acids in living matter. Many people in the academic circles that Francis Crick ran in thought of him as one of the artistic men in science, so as he aged and his beliefs and research became more and more abstract, they were shocked.

Out of the many strange theories he put forward, maybe one of Crick's weirdest ideas was the one he released in the

1970s. Crick started advocating the pseudo-scientific theory of directed panspermia. Religious occultists had touted this theory during the 60s, and soon Crick started meeting with some of these occultists to discuss this theory.

Directed panspermia is the theory that all life on earth was created on purpose by beings from other worlds who seeded the earth. This theory then discusses how microorganisms could be transported into space and be used on other planets to create life. Some of Crick's contemporaries would go on to say that this process could be used to seed other systems or even star-forming clouds with microorganisms to build a wider web of organic life forms.

Though Francis Crick's research brought us one of the most important finds in the 20th century, his wild speculations of otherworldly creators affected his reputation throughout the remainder of his life.

The Scientist & The Occultist

Though NASA history may have written the name Jack Parsons out of its history books, it is undeniable that he still played a pivotal role in the invention of the rocket engine and liquid fuel rockets. Jack Parsons was a rocket engineer and chemist that worked for Caltech during the 30s and 40s. He would go on to be a founding member of Jet Propulsion and Aerojet engineering corporation, both of which played a role in the founding of NASA.

Sadly for Jack, his curiosity didn't only have to do with science but also communism and the occult. His moral code was called into question because of his interest in these movements and his propensity for extramarital dalliances. The questioning of his morals is what urged NASA to remove him from its historical records.

The story of Jack Parsons is something right out of a Hollywood movie. Hard at work at researching and developing new rocket technology in 1939, Jack found a new religious movement that seemed to fit his ideology. This movement was called the Lima, and it was founded by the famous English occultist Aleister Crowley.

Both Parsons and his wife quickly joined the lodge in California and became dedicated members. Jack would take over the lodge in 1942, and just two years later, he found himself removed from the boards of both JPL and Aerojet because of the religious reputation of this branch.

Some of the branches alleged practices like dancing nude around a fire in a garden and practicing other Pagan rituals had become common knowledge, which offended many of the other members of the boards. Through his rise in the order, Jack became close friends with the occultist Aleister Crowley, and he would soon be joined by other famous names.

Jack would also befriend an up-and-coming author who would go on to create his own "religious" order known as Scientology. L. Ron Hubbard and Jack became close friends, even sharing some very personal time together in the lodge.

The two would begin experimenting in ways that even Aleister Crowley felt were a little outside the box. They would attempt to summon spirits and even share mistresses. In fact, Hubbard would eventually leave the order, taking Parsons girlfriend with him.

Parsons lived an exciting life, but in the end, his love for science and the occult would be the death of him. Just days before he was set to head out to Mexico on vacation, Parsons felt he had to do one more experiment. On June 17th, 1952, Parsons disappeared into his home laboratory. Soon after, there was a loud explosion, and the building was blown to bits. It took authorities a little while to get through the debris and when they did they came upon a sight that seemed right out of a horror film. Parsons body was found, his face almost completely gone as well as most of his bones shattered, and his right arm was missing from the elbow down.

Jack Parsons, a brilliant yet disturbed mind, tragically lost his life by his own hands.

Electricity War?

When most people learn about electricity in school, two names are synonymous with the topic—Nikola Tesla and Thomas Edison. Thanks to Hollywood, many now know that war waged between the two for many years regarding current electricity that should be used. To understand this war, you have to go back to the very beginning of their relationship.

Nikola Tesla worked his way up the ladder and moved to France, where he worked for a company affiliated with Thomas Edison. After showing his worth there, he moved to the United States to work with Edison one-on-one.

Edison had already patented the lightbulb by the time Tesla came to work with him and was beginning to control the current electricity. This project would cause the two to eventually fall out, with Edison touting direct current to answer the problem and Tesla favoring an alternating current.

Soon, Tesla would prove to Edison that his option was not only inefficient but more expensive. This would lead to the two going their separate ways and finding funding from rival financial companies. Edison would partner with JP Morgan, and Tesla, who finally created his own electric company, and would be backed by George Westinghouse Jr.

Tesla's company started out with a bang, but Edison had the media coverage after some fatal accidents tarnished Tesla and his company's reputation. This "current war" would eventually wind up being a propaganda war of which Edison was the clear winner. Even though Edison won the war, destiny changed its course and the country opted to use Tesla's alternating current system. Regrettably for Tesla, he had sold his patents to Westinghouse and earned nothing from his hard work.

Eventually, Edison would go on to register over one thousand patents and have his hand in home appliances and the film industry. His diversification made him and his company, now called General Electric, one of the biggest companies in the country.

On the other hand, after Tesla's loss during the current war, he ended up penniless and mad. He would die alone and ridiculed because of his eccentric research projects and communing with aliens.

The Bishop And A Lunar Civilization

Man has stared into the skies for centuries and wondered what was beyond the shining lights There were plenty of people who had ideas of sailing among the stars many years before man would be able to get out and explore the skies in the 20th century. Perhaps one of the very first that laid out their ideas in public was Dr. John Wilkins.

Dr. John Wilkins began dreaming and planning how a man could find his way into space in 1640. He dreamed of a winged chariot that was able to escape the pressure of gravity and sail through the stars and land on the moon where a civilization would be there to meet him. Wilkins, unlike many of his religious contemporaries, believed that anything was possible. With many other people studying the stars and planets like Galileo, his love for outer space grew exponentially.

He had been mulling over this theory for quite a while. He thought about this so much that he released a book in 1638, discussing how he thought it was possible to reach the stars. This book delved into the theories of how the moon had inhabitants on it and how more civilizations could be built on the moon in the future. This book was what he used to show to potential investors he was trying to gain to help him make his dreams come true.

With every proposal, he had to break down how certain things would be handled, such as diet and sleep when landing on the moon. Wilkins wasn't the only person at this time looking into theories about alien lifeforms and space travel though. This allowed Wilkins to engage in intellectual conversations with them and expand upon his ideas. These relationships would eventually lead to him and other natural philosophers founding the Royal Society of Science in England.

Many believe all of his theories were simply ideas and nothing more. There were also some rumors that some of the experiments actually made it into the testing phase.

Regrettably, the science didn't make it up to the speed it needed to have any of his theories come to fruition.

Being the dreamer that he is, Wilkins made do with the limited 17th century technology that he had. He continued to work on his quest to propel humans into space until his last breath.

Fleece As White As Snow

Every child knows about the famous nursery rhyme from 1830, *Mary Had a Little Lamb*. Though it is a simple tale, parents and teachers who sang this nursery rhyme to children helped it last for more than a century. Unlike many nursery rhymes and other stories, this cute but short story is actually based on fact.

The real-life Mary was born in 1806, in Sterling, Massachusetts. Mary Elizabeth Sawyer, like many other kids at the time, grew up on a farm. Going about her day doing her chores, she came across a newborn lamb that had been left and was quite sick. The young, compassionate Mary took the time to nurse it back to health. It didn't take long for the lamb to gain its total health back. The lamb became attached to Mary because of this, and would follow her everywhere she went.

The lamb soon became Mary's best friend and constant companion, and followed her to school on numerous occasions. Getting to class, Mary noticed that teacher had not arrived, and so she snuck the lamb in and placed it under her desk, covering it with a blanket. For quite a while, the lamb lay quietly under the desk, but when Mary stood up to recite something in front of the class, the lamb followed her like it always did. This reveal was shocking to both the teacher and the rest of the class.

The unamused teacher made Mary take the lamb outside and tie it up until class was over. One of the students in the class thought this was a funny situation and quickly wrote a small poem that he would give to Mary the next day.

Though the original poem is not the one recited in classrooms and homes across the globe, the version all people know is definitely taken from that anecdote.

Pepsi & Its Private Army

There are many different kinds of soda, but the considerable debate is whether an individual prefers Coca-Cola or Pepsi. This choice can depend on where a person lives in the United States or even the country they came from. But when someone thinks of the fizzy drink, you don't necessarily think of a private army. Nevertheless, there was a time in history when Pepsi had control over the 6th largest navy in the world. How did that happen? It was because the Soviet Union and Russia had a devoted love for this carbonated beverage.

The Soviet Union learned about Pepsi during a meeting between the then Vice President Nixon and the Soviet leader Khrushchev in 1959. In a friendly debate about capitalism versus communism, things began to get a little heated, so

Nixon offered Khrushchev a Pepsi. Once the communist leader had a sip, he was hooked.

Pepsi's popularity spread from there, and several years later, the Soviet Union decided they wanted to broker a deal with Pepsi to allow their products into the country. Unfortunately, the Russian currency was not accepted globally, so the Soviet Union had to get a little creative. They had to find something that they had that everybody in the world wanted. At the time, their first thought went straight to vodka. After all, who doesn't want an excellent traditional Russian vodka? The transaction went through, and Pepsi became the only American soda allowed to enter the Soviet Union. The contract wasn't forever, and in the late 1980s, it came up for negotiation.

Regrettably for the Russians, Pepsi's original agreement with their government wasn't going to be enough. Panicked, the Russians began to throw out ideas of how they could pay for an extended right to have Pepsi in their country. They eventually brokered a deal with Pepsi—the Russians were willing to give a whole fleet of submarines and boats for a large quantity of soda.

Pepsi was given seventeen submarines, a frigate, a cruiser, and a destroyer in this agreement. These ships equaled about three billion dollars. This is how Pepsi became the sixth most powerful military in the world.

Pepsi turned around and sold the vessels and submarines to the Swedes to scrap for recycling so their reign as a military force was short lived.

Canada & Denmark At War

There are many places where borders between two countries come into question. Many times these questions lead to conflicts, most of which remain unknown.

Take for instance, the conflict of Hans Island between Canada and Denmark. This island is situated in the Kennedy Channel between Greenland and Ellesmere Island. Because the border ran straight down the Kennedy Channel, there is a line in the middle of the island separating the half that belonged to Canada and the other half that belonged to Denmark. This situation caused some friction between the countries in 1973, when a border treaty was signed, leaving a gap in the border description.

For a little over a decade, the two nations peacefully coexisted, but in 1984, a Canadian decided to plant a flag with a bottle of whiskey next to it on the island. This move angered the Danish minister of Greenland, who hopped on a boat and journeyed out to the island that same year. When the minister arrived, he placed a Danish flag and left a bottle of schnapps and a little letter welcoming people to the Danish island. For decades, the countries exchanged claims to the island back and forth, including military landings and letters of protest.

Finally, in 2005, the two countries agreed to go through a process that would eventually resolve the issue. By 2012, a proposal to simply split the island in half was presented to Denmark and Canada. Within that same year, a couple of months after the proposal had been submitted, both countries finally agreed on the exact border after decades of conflict.

This proposal marked the end of the conflict now known as the Whiskey War.

The Indestructible Man

The war had been waging for several years and had spread throughout the world, including Europe and the Pacific front. North America was looking to end the conflict in the Pacific. They turned to a new weapon that would devastate their enemy and allow them to gain the upper hand.

During WWII, there had been many advancements, and one of those was the atomic bomb. When America decided to use this devastating weapon, they targeted two major cities on the island nation of Japan. When all was said and done, two hundred sixty thousand people survived the explosions, but many survivors were left with injuries and lifelong health problems.

When the images of the bombs are played in documentaries, it is hard to believe that there were any survivors, let alone someone who survived both of the bombs. But there are individuals like Tsutomu Yamaguchi, who survived both Hiroshima and Nagasaki.

Yamaguchi was a naval engineer staying in Hiroshima for three months on a business trip for Mitsubishi Heavy Industries. August 6, 1945, was his last day in this city, and Yamaguchi was preparing to leave. Making his final rounds that very morning, he heard an aircraft in the distance overhead. He quickly looked up and saw an American bomber flying over the city and watched as a small object dropped from its underbelly. Within seconds the bomb exploded, and there was a bright light and a loud boom. The shockwave that came with it pulled Yamaguchi down and flung him across the ground. With bad burns and ruptured eardrums, Yamaguchi stumbled towards the shipyard. He found an air raid shelter and curled up for the night, eventually realizing he and the other survivors had to find a way out of the city. When the following day broke, they worked their way to a train and began their journey back home to Nagasaki.

The train with Yamaguchi finally arrived on August 8th, and he made his way slowly to the hospital. Once he had been treated, Yamaguchi left the hospital and returned to work the next day. Unfortunately for him, he was to experience a much more powerful explosion than he did in Hiroshima. When the bomb dropped, Yamaguchi was in his office. Though the boom was muffled, the force that hit him was strong enough to blow the bandages off and expose him to more radiation than he had in the initial blast. Struggling to get up, he found his way out of the Mitsubishi building and headed home to check on his family.

Yamaguchi found his family and over the next few days, he began to fall ill. He lost his hair, and his arms turned gangrenous, and he became very sick. On August 15, Emperor Hirohito surrendered, and the war for Japan was over.

Fortunately for Yamaguchi, the side effects of the radiation and atomic explosion subsided eventually, and he became one of the only people to survive both nuclear blasts.

The Ship's Going Down Again!?

The tragic tale of the Titanic has been told time and again, both in history classes and on the silver screen. It is a tale that everyone knows, but only a few know about the stories of the people who were on board the ship. One of the most interesting stories is probably the tale of Violet Jessop, a woman who survived the sinking of the Titanic and two other ships.

Violet Jessop was born in 1887, in Argentina, and was one of six children. Her family had immigrated to Argentina from Ireland in search of a better life. Violet lived a turbulent life in her youth, almost succumbing to tuberculosis at an early age. But survive she did, and at twenty-three, decided that she needed to follow her own path. By 1910, Violet signed up as a stewardess for the White Star line. Her first appointment would be at the RMS Olympic. Unfortunately, this assignment did not last long for the Olympic soon ran into a British warship, the HMS Hawk. Though neither ship actually sank, they definitely took on water, and this was the first of her three triumphs over tragedy.

For many, this harrowing brush with death would have scared them off of the idea of traveling the open seas on a luxury cruiser, but Violet Jessop decided to sign back up and be a part of the crew for a great new ship called the RMS Titanic. On April 14, 1912, Jessup set out just like every other passenger on the Titanic to cross the ocean. Sadly, during this voyage, the ship struck an iceberg and began to sink. Violet Jessop was one of the lucky ones who got onto a lifeboat. She floated away from the sinking vessel along with several children. Eventually, Jessop and the other survivors were picked up by the Carpathia and taken to safety.

Violet's brush with death was very close this time, yet she still found her way onto another vessel, the HMHS Britannic. This vessel, too, was a White Star liner that had been used as a hospital ship during the war. Just fifty-five minutes after leaving port there was a loud explosion, and the ship began to sink.

At twenty-nine, Violet Jessop had survived three near catastrophes with death, all while trying to travel the world on the seas.

Conclusion

Strange and obscure things in nature and history have captivated people for centuries. After all, anything that can pull them out of the mundane and give their life a bit of mysticism and intrigue is a much needed distraction from their woes and tribulations.

Good thing there are weird stories in almost every sphere of interest. From the doctor who tried to sell a modern-day condiment as medicine to the building of an entire fake city to relieve the pressures of war, these are just a few of the weirdest stories throughout history.

References

Rowley, Jim; Weird Historical Stories That Sound Made Up (But Aren't) (December 2020) Retrieved from https://www.ranker.com/list/historical-weird-true-stories/jim-rowley

Hughes, Virginia; The Tragic Story of How Einstein's Brain was Stolen and Wasn't Even Special (April 2014) Retrieved from https://www.nationalgeographic.com/science/article/the-tragic-story-of-how-einsteins-brain-was-stolen-and-wasnt-even-special

Xaviery; The Story of How Albert Einstein's Brain Was Stolen (September 2020) Retrieved from https://historyofyesterday.com/the-story-of-how-albert-einsteins-brain-was-stolen-a17b93ee1b7f

Harper Elizabeth; The Cadaver Synod: When A Pope's Corpse Was Put On Trial (March 2014) Retrieved from https://www.atlasobscura.com/articles/morbid-monday-cadaver-synod

Britannia Editors; Cadaver Synod; Retrieved from https://www.britannica.com/topic/Cadaver-Synod

Kruse, Colton; Cadaver Synod: The Trial of Pope Formosus's Corpse (February 2020) Retrieved from https://www.ripleys.com/weird-news/cadaver-synod/

Greenspan, Jesse; The Confederacy Made Its Last Stand In Brazil (June 2020) Retrieved from https://www.history.com/news/confederacy-in-brazil-civil-war

Dunn Morgan; Meet The Confederados The Confederate Loyalists Who Fled To Brazil After The Civil War (July 2020) Retried from https://allthatsinteresting.com/confederados

Mimi Dwyer; The Brazilian Town Where The American Confederacy Lives On (February 2015) Retrieved from https://www.vice.com/en/article/gq8ae9/welcome-to-americana-brazil-0000580-v22n2

Patowary Kaushik; The Most Kissed Girl In The World: The Mona Lisa od The Seine (September 2018) Retrieved from https://www.amusingplanet.com/2018/09/the-most-kissed-girl-in-world-mona-lisa.html

Brightside Editors; How An unknown Girl From Paris Got The Most Kissed Lips In History; Retrieved from https://brightside.me/wonder-curiosities/how-an-unknown-girl-from-paris-got-the-most-kissed-lips-in-history-794621/

The Star Writers; The Most Kissed Girl In The World (December 2020) Retrieved from https://www.thestar.com.my/lifestyle/health/2020/12/23/the-most-kissed-girl-in-the-world

Matthews, Dylan; 7 Bizarre Ways The US Tried To Kill Or Topple Fidel Castro (November 2016) Retrieved from https://www.vox.com/2016/11/26/13752514/us-fidel-castro-assassination

Smith, Alexander; Fidel Castro: The CIA's 7 Most Bizarre Assassination Attempts (November 2016) Retrieved from https://www.nbcnews.com/storyline/fidel-castros-death/fidel-castro-cia-s-7-most-bizarre-assassination-attempts-n688951

Campbell, Duncan; Close But No Cigar: How America Failed To Kill Fidel Castro (November 2016) Retrieved from https://www.theguardian.com/world/2016/nov/26/fidel-castro-cia-cigar-assasination-attempts

Greenspan, Jesse; The Assassination of Archduke Franz Ferdinand (February 2020) Retrieved from https://www.history.com/news/the-assassination-of-archduke-franz-ferdinand

MacMillan, Margaret; The Archduke's Assassination Came Close To Being Just Another Killing (June 2014) Retrieved from https://www.theglobeandmail.com/news/world/how-the-archdukes-assassination-came-close-to-being-just-another-killing/article19379097/

White, Frances; The Nearly Botched Assassination of Franz Ferdinand (April 2015) Retrieved from https://www.historyanswers.co.uk/people-politics/the-nearly-botched-assassination-of-franz-ferdinand/

Andrews, Evan; World War II's Bizarre 'Battle of Los Angeles' (May 2020) Retrieved from https://www.history.com/news/world-war-iis-bizarre-battle-of-los-angeles

Harrison Scott; From the Archives: The 1942 Battle of L.A. (February 2017) Retrieved from https://www.latimes.com/visuals/framework/la-me-fw-archives-1942-battle-la-20170221-story.html

Wikipedia; Battle of Los Angeles (July 2021) Retrieved from https://en.wikipedia.org/wiki/Battle_of_Los_Angeles

Nix, Elizabeth; Did An Apple Really Fall On Isaac Newton's Head? (September 2018) Retrieved from https://www.history.com/news/did-an-apple-really-fall-on-isaac-newtons-head

Author Unknown; The Legend of Newton's Apple Tree (March 2021) Retrieved from https://www.bbvaopenmind.com/en/science/physics/legend-of-newtons-apple-tree/

Gefter, Amanda; Newton's Apple: The Real Story (January 2010) Retrieved from https://www.newscientist.com/article/2170052-newtons-apple-the-real-story/

Brumfiel, Geoff; Total Failure: The World's Worst Video Game (May 2017) Retrieved from https://www.npr.org/2017/05/31/530235165/total-failure-the-worlds-worst-video-game

Kleinman, Jake; The Worst Video Game of All Tie Got One Thing Hilariously Right (October 2020) Retrieved from https://www.inverse.com/gaming/et-atari-game-history-review

Lee, Helen A.; Why E.T. Is Considered The 'Worst Video Game In History' (August 2020) Retrieved from https://www.looper.com/242031/why-e-t-is-considered-the-worst-video-game-in-history/

Ouellette, Jennifer; That Time Benjamin Franklin Tried (And Failed) To Electrocute A Turkey (November 2019) Retrieved from https://arstechnica.com/science/2019/11/that-time-benjamin-franklin-tried-and-failed-to-electrocute-a-turkey/

Marsh, Allison; Ben Franklin's Other Great Electrical Discovery: Turkey Tenderization (November 2018) Retrieved from https://spectrum.ieee.org/tech-history/dawn-of-electronics/ben-franklins-iotheri-great-electrical-discovery-turkey-tenderization

Tretkoff, Ernie; This Month In Physics History: Ben Franklin Attempts To Electrocute A Turkey (December 2006) Retrieved from https://www.aps.org/publications/apsnews/200612/history.cfm

Grande, Sabana; The US Government Intentionally Poisoned Alcohol During the Prohibition (February 2020) Retrieved from https://medium.com/lessons-from-history/the-u-s-government-intentionally-poisoned-alcohol-during-the-prohibition-f39d6bd427be

Lopez, German; The US Government One Poisoned Alcohol To get People to Stop Drinking (August 2014) Retrieved from https://www.vox.com/2014/8/8/5975605/alcohol-prohibition-poison

Blum, Deborah; The Chemist's War: The Little-told Story of How the US Government Poisoned Alcohol During the Prohibition With Deadly Consequences (February 2010) Retrieved from https://slate.com/technology/2010/02/the-little-told-story-of-how-the-u-s-government-poisoned-alcohol-during-prohibition.html

Klein, Christopher; When Massachusetts Banned Christmas (December 2020) Retrieved from https://www.history.com/news/when-massachusetts-banned-christmas

Doe, Martha; The Puritan Ban On Christmas (2005) Retrieved from https://www.timetravel-britain.com/articles/christmas/ban.shtml

Tourgee Heather; How the Puritans Banned Christmas (December 2020) Retrieved from https://newengland.com/today/living/new-england-history/how-the-puritans-banned-christmas/

Summers, Megan; The Strange Death of Harry Houdini: Accident – Or Murder? (April 2020) Retrieved from https://filmdaily.co/news/harry-houdini-death/

Andrews, Evan; What Killed Harry Houdini? (August 2018) Retrieved from https://www.history.com/news/what-killed-harry-houdini

Markel, Dr. Howard; What caused Harry Houdini's Mysterious Death? (March 2019) Retrieved from https://www.pbs.org/newshour/health/what-caused-harry-houdinis-mysterious-death#:~:text=After%20a%20second%20operation%20on,at%20the%20age%20of%2052.

Niiler, Eric; Hitler Sent A Secret Expedition To Antarctica In A Hunt For Margarine Fat (August 2018) Retrieved from https://www.pbs.org/newshour/health/what-caused-harry-houdinis-mysterious-death#:~:text=After%20a%20second%20operation%20on,at%20the%20age%20of%2052.

Fater, Luke; Hitler's Secret Antarctic Expedition For Whales (November 2019) Retrieved from https://www.atlasobscura.com/articles/nazis-in-antarctica

Wikipedia; New Swabia (June 2021) Retrieved from https://en.wikipedia.org/wiki/New_Swabia#:~:text=were%20drawn%20up.-,German%20Antarctic%20Expedition%20(1938%E2%80%931939),increase%20Germany's%20production%20of%20fat.

Barrett, Claire; Hiroo Onoda, The Japanese Officer Who Refused To Surrender Decades After WWII's End (October 2020) Retrieved from https://www.historynet.com/hiroo-onoda-the-japanese-officer-who-refused-to-surrender-decades-after-wwiis-end.htm

Author Unknown; Japan WW2 Soldier Who Refused To Surrender Hiroo Onoda Dies (January 2014) Retrieved from https://www.bbc.com/news/world-asia-25772192

Arbuckle, Alex Q., The Soldier Who Wouldn't Surrender Hiroo Onoda Fought On For Three Decades; Retrieved from https://mashable.com/feature/hiroo-onoda

Andrews, Evan; Did George Washington Have Wooden Teeth? (February 2020) Retrieved from https://www.history.com/news/did-george-washington-have-wooden-teeth

Pappas, Stephanie; What Were George Washington's Teeth Made Of? (It's Not Wood) (March 2018) Retrieved from https://www.livescience.com/61919-george-washington-teeth-not-wood.html

Wills, Matthew; Were George Washington's Teeth Taken From Enslaved People? (February 2020) Retrieved from https://daily.jstor.org/were-george-washingtons-teeth-taken-from-enslaved-people/

Clark, Stuart; Apocalypse Postponed: How Earth Survived Halley's Comet In 1910 (December 2012) Retrieved from https://www.theguardian.com/science/across-the-universe/2012/dec/20/apocalypse-postponed-halley-comet

Chavers, Penny; Halley's Comet Panic Of 1910 (August 2019) Retrieved from https://curioushistorian.com/halleys-comet-panic-of-1910

Simon, Matt; Fantastically Wrong: That Time People Thought A Comet Would Gas Us All To Death (January 2015) Retrieved from https://www.wired.com/2015/01/fantastically-wrong-halleys-comet/

Author Unknown; The Mystery of John Glenn's Fireflies Returns; Retrieved from https://www.universetoday.com/82211/the-mystery-of-john-glenns-fireflies-returns/

Maranzani, Barbara; 7 Things you May Not Know About John Glenn (December 2016) Retrieved from https://www.history.com/news/7-things-you-may-notknow-about-john-glenn-and-friendship-7

Hlavaty, Craig; The Story Behind the 'Fireflies' That Astronaut John Glenn Saw In Space (February 2019) Retrieved from https://www.chron.com/news/nation-world/article/The-story-behind-astronaut-John-Glenn-s-10783488.php

Moore, Nolan; The Real Stories Behind Bizarre Events In History (October 2016) Retrieved from https://www.grunge.com/29108/real-stories-behind-bizarre-events-history/

Pruitt, Sarah; The Riddle of Edgar Allan Poe's Death (October 2015) Retrieved from https://www.history.com/news/how-did-edgar-allan-poe-die

Geiling, Natasha; The (Still) Mysterious Death of Edgar Allan Poe (October 2014) Retrieved from https://www.smithsonianmag.com/history/still-mysterious-death-edgar-allan-poe-180952936/

Zakarin, Jordan; Why Edgar Allan Poe's Death Remains A Mystery (October 2020) Retrieved from https://www.biography.com/news/edgar-allan-poe-death

History.com Editors; The Mary Celeste, A Ship Whose Crew Mysteriously Disappeared While At Sea (July 2021) Retrieved from https://www.history.com/this-day-in-history/the-mystery-of-the-mary-celeste

Pruitt, Sarah; What Happened To The Mary Celeste? (July 2021) Retrieved from https://www.history.com/news/what-happened-to-the-mary-celeste

Blumberg, Jess; Abandoned Ship: The Mary Celeste (November 2007) Retrieved from https://www.smithsonianmag.com/history/abandoned-ship-the-mary-celeste-174488104/

Sakthivel, Adithya Vikram; The Angels of Mons: From Myth to Fact (November 2018) Retrieved from https://historyhub.info/the-angel-of-mons-from-myth-to-fact/

Brigden, James; The Angel of Mons And Other Supernatural Stories From WWII; Retrieved from https://www.history.co.uk/articles/the-angel-of-mons-and-other-strange-supernatural-stories-from-world-war-i

Coulson, Alan S.; The Case Of The Elusive Angel Of Mons; Retrieved from http://www.worldwar1.com/heritage/angel.htm

Unknown Author; The Mad Gasser Of Mattoon; Retrieved from https://www.americanhauntingsink.com/madgasser

Otiode Monica; The Mad Gasser of Mattoon (August 2019) Retrieved from https://www.library.illinois.edu/hpnl/blog/the-mad-gasser-of-mattoon/

Wikipedia; Mad Gasser of Mattoon (July 2021) Retrieved from https://en.wikipedia.org/wiki/Mad_Gasser_of_Mattoon

Shorter, Edward; The First Psychiatric Pandemic: Encephalitis Lethargica, 1917 -27 (January 2021) Retrieved from https://pubmed.ncbi.nlm.nih.gov/33268001/

Moawad, Heidi (MD); Encephalitis Lethargica: The Still Unexplained Sleeping Sickness (February 2018) Retrieved from https://www.neurologylive.com/view/encephalitis-lethargica-still-unexplained-sleeping-sickness

Hoffman, Leslie A. & Vilensky, Joel A.; Encephalitis Lethargica: 100 Years After The Epidemic (August 2017) Retrieved from https://academic.oup.com/brain/article/140/8/2246/3970828

Bocco, Diana; The Curious Case Of Mercy Brown And The New England Vampire Panic (July 2016) Retrieved from https://www.ripleys.com/weird-news/the-curious-case-of-mercy-brown-and-the-new-england-vampire-panic/

Author Unknown; Did Vampires Really Stalk Ne3w England Farm Families?; Retrieved from https://www.newenglandhistoricalsociety.com/did-vampires-really-stalk-new-england-farm-families/

Tucker, Abigail; The Great New England Vampire Panic (October 2012) Retrieved from https://www.smithsonianmag.com/history/the-great-new-england-vampire-panic-36482878/

White, Edward; An Extraordinary Delivery of Rabbits (July 2016) Retrieved from https://www.theparisreview.org/blog/2016/07/05/an-extraordinary-delivery-of-rabbits/

Imbler, Sabrina; Why Historians Are Reexamining the Case of the Woman Who Gave Birth To Rabbits (July 2019) Retrieved from https://www.atlasobscura.com/articles/mary-toft-gave-birth-to-rabbits

Bell, Beth; The Woman Who Gave Birth To Rabbits (And Other Hoaxes) (March 2018) Retrieved from https://www.bbc.com/news/uk-england-43073391

Johnson, Ben; The Shortest War In History; Retrieved from
https://www.historic-uk.com/HistoryUK/HistoryofBritain/The-Shortest-
War-in-History/

Pollard, Justin & Stephanie; The Anglo-Zanzibar War (August 2018)
Retrieved from https://www.historytoday.com/archive/months-
past/anglo-zanzibar-war

Author Unknown; Shortest war Of All Time (February 2021) Retrieved
from https://www.military.com/video/shortest-war-of-all-time-anglo-
zanzibar-war-one-minute-history

Karuga, James; Did You Know Albert Einstein Was Offered The Israeli
Presidency? (May 2017) Retrieved from
https://www.worldatlas.com/articles/did-you-know-albert-einstein-was-
offered-the-israeli-presidency.html

Unknown Author; Israel: Einstein Declines (December 1952) Retrieved
from
http://content.time.com/time/subscriber/article/0,33009,817454,00.html

Fan, Ryan; Why Albert Einstein Rejected Being President of Israel
(October 2020) Retrieved from https://medium.com/frame-of-
reference/why-albert-einstein-rejected-being-president-of-israel-
7d5acc7280a6

Then, Ker; King Tit Mysteries Solved: Was Disabled Malarial, and
Inbred (February 2010) Retrieved from
https://www.nationalgeographic.com/culture/article/100216-king-tut-
malaria-bones-inbred-tutankhamun

History.com Editors; Tutankhamun (July 2020) Retrieved from
https://www.history.com/topics/ancient-history/tutankhamen

Author Unknown; Tutankhamun's Parents Were cousins, Not Siblings (
February 2013) Retrieved from
https://timesofindia.indiatimes.com/home/science/tutankhamun-parents-
were-cousins-not-siblings/articleshow/18584107.cms

Raspberry, Hossein; 7 Historical Facts That Are Too Weird and Crazy to
Believe (October 2020) Retrieved from https://historyofyesterday.com/7-
historical-facts-that-are-too-weird-and-crazy-to-believe-96d0b5df26d7

Flannagan, S.; These Three Dictators Were Nominated For The Nobel Peace Prize (July 2021) Retrieved from https://www.grunge.com/452780/these-three-dictators-were-nominated-for-the-nobel-peace-prize/

Mendes, Claudia; The Irony – Nobel Peace Prize Nominees Include Hitler, Stalin and Mussolini (February 2019) Retrieved from https://www.warhistoryonline.com/instant-articles/nobel-peace-prize-nominees.html

Moura, Ana Isabel; Hitler, Stalin, and Mussolini Were Nominated For The Nobel Peace Prize (February 2021) Retrieved from https://primetimezone.com/world/hitler-stalin-and-mussolini-were-nominated-for-the-nobel-peace-prize/

Crawford, Amy; Who Was Cleopatra? (March 2007) Retrieved from https://www.smithsonianmag.com/history/who-was-cleopatra-151356013/

Andrews, Evan; 10 Little-Known Facts About Cleopatra (April 2021) Retrieved from https://www.history.com/news/10-little-known-facts-about-cleopatra

Chakraborty, Rakhi; Torches of Freedom: How The World's First PR Campaign Came To Be (August 2014) Retrieved from https://yourstory.com/2014/08/torches-of-freedom/amp

Mostegel, Iris; The Original Influencer (February 2019) Retrieved from https://www.historytoday.com/miscellanies/original-influencer

Amos, Amanda & Haglund, Margaretha; From Social Taboo to "Torch of Freedom": The Marketing of Cigarettes To Women; Retrieved from https://tobaccocontrol.bmj.com/content/9/1/3

Unknown Author; Workshop Scholar Sets Record For world's Longest History Lesson (August 2018) Retrieved from https://www.humanitiestexas.org/news/articles/workshop-scholar-sets-record-worlds-longest-history-lesson

Unknown Author; Longest History Lesson (August 2018) Retrieved from https://www.guinnessworldrecords.com/world-records/487570-longest-history-lesson

214

Mark, Joshua J., The First Labor Strike (July 2017) Retrieved from
https://www.worldhistory.org/article/1089/the-first-labor-strike-in-history/

Unknown Author; First Recorded Strike; Retrieved from
https://www.guinnessworldrecords.com/world-records/first-recorded-strike

Duducu, Jem; 7 Moments in History you (Might) Think Are Made Up
But Aren't (August 2015) Retrieved from
https://www.historyextra.com/period/ancient-egypt/7-moments-in-history-you-might-think-are-made-up-but-arent/

Crimecapsule; Murder Ballads: Love, Lust, and Legend in the Blue Ridge
Mountains (April 2020) Retrieved from https://crimecapsule.com/murder-ballads-love-lust-and-legend-in-the-blue-ridge-mountains/

Chimesfreedom; The True Story of Tom Dooley; Retrieved from
http://www.chimesfreedom.com/2017/11/17/true-story-tom-dooley/

Unknown Author; The Legend Behind North Carolina's Most Famous
Murder Ballad (October 2019) Retrieved from
https://www.ncarts.org/comehearnc/365-days-music/legend-behind-north-carolina%E2%80%99s-most-famous-murder-ballad

Edwards, Charlotte; Rock Bottom World's Deepest Hoe Dubbed 'Well to
Hell Plunges 40,000 feet – and Is Only Covered by Rusty Soviet metal
Lid (August 2019) Retrieved from
https://www.thesun.co.uk/tech/9786114/worlds-deepest-hole-well-to-hell/

Wiles, James; The Fascinating Truth Behind The "Well To Hell" Hoax
(July 2017) Retrieved from https://www.urbo.com/content/the-fascinating-truth-behind-the-well-to-hell-hoax/

Mikkelson, Barbara; The Well To Hell (December 1998) Retrieved from
https://www.snopes.com/fact-check/the-well-to-hell/

Author Unknown; Issei Sagawa; Retrieved from
https://murderpedia.org/male.S/s/sagawa-issei.htm

Tullos, Amanda; The Horrifying True Story Of Issei Sagawa: The
Celebrity Cannibal (June 2016) Retrieved from

http://www.the13thfloor.tv/2016/06/10/the-horrifying-true-story-of-issei-sagawa-the-celebrity-cannibal/

Bartlette, DeLani R.; Issei Sagawa: The Celebrity Cannibal (November 2020) Retrieved from https://delanirbartlette.medium.com/issei-sagawa-the-celebrity-cannibal-a78c90255be6

Wong, Stacy; Taking the Sting Out of the 'Killer Bee' Myths (April 1993) Retrieved from https://www.latimes.com/archives/la-xpm-1993-04-15-me-23222-story.html

Herman, Marc; Stop Trying To Make Killer Bees Happen (July 2017) Retrieved from https://psmag.com/social-justice/stop-trying-make-killer-bees-happen-68087

Harris, Karen; The 'Killer Bees' Scare Of The '70s: Was There A Real Threat? (July 2018) Retrieved from https://groovyhistory.com/killer-bees-1970s

Author Unknown; Who Killed Superman? (November 2006) Retrieved from https://www.theguardian.com/film/2006/nov/18/features.weekend1

Dimuro, Gina; Who Killed Superman George Reeves? (February 2018) Retrieved from https://allthatsinteresting.com/george-reeves-superman

Heim, Bec; Was Superman Murdered? The Mysterious Death of George Reeves (April 2020) Retrieved from https://filmdaily.co/news/george-reeves/

Miller, Madison; 'All in the Family': Who Was the 'Real-Life Archie Bunker? (February 2021) Retrieved from https://outsider.com/news/entertainment/all-in-the-family-who-was-real-life-archie-bunker/

Gross, Ed; 'All in the Family' Was Based on Britain's 'Till Death Us Do Part' – Meet the Original Bunkers (January 2021) Retrieved from https://doyouremember.com/141136/all-in-the-family-till-death-us-do-part

Dorwart, Laura; 'All in the Family': Who Was the Character Archie Bunker Based On? (December 2020) Retrieved from https://www.cheatsheet.com/entertainment/all-in-the-family-who-was-the-character-of-archie-bunker-based-on.html/

Krajick, Kevin; Fire in the Hole(May 2005) Retrieved from https://www.smithsonianmag.com/science-nature/fire-in-the-hole-77895126/

Baker, Sinead & Spector, Dina; This US Town Has Been Abandoned or Almost 60 Years Because of an Underground Fire That continues To Burn (September 2019) Retrieved from https://www.businessinsider.com/photos-of-centralia-pennsylvania-burning-coal-town-2011-11

Blakemore, Erin; This Mine Has Been Burning For Over 50 Years (April 2019) Retrieved from https://www.history.com/news/mine-fire-burning-more-50-years-ghost-town

Warden, Rob; Elvis Volunteered to Inform For the FBI, 1970 Memo Says (July 1978) Retrieved from https://www.washingtonpost.com/archive/politics/1978/07/14/elvis-volunteered-to-inform-for-the-fbi-1970-memo-says/6ab4bf40-e31b-4a3d-a4aa-580e6e60abcf/

Blazeski, Goran; Elvis Presley Asks President Nixon To Make Him An FBI Special Agent (November 2016) Retrieved from https://www.thevintagenews.com/2016/11/04/elvis-presley-asks-president-nixon-to-make-him-an-fbi-special-agent/

Nguyen Stacy; The New Smiley Face Killers Movie Is Loosely Based On The Hotly Contested Theory (December 2020) Retrieved from https://www.popsugar.com/entertainment/what-is-smiley-face-killer-theory-48046699

Vanbaale, Kali White; Are The Smiley Face Murders Real? (December 2020) Retrieved from https://www.aetv.com/real-crime/are-the-smiley-face-killers-real

Hayden, Aly Vander; 5 Chilling Details That Will Make You Believe In The 'Smiley Face Killings' (January 2019) Retrieved from https://www.oxygen.com/crime-time/chilling-details-make-you-believe-smiley-face-killings

Davis, Miriam; The Axeman of New Orleans Preyed On Italian Immigrants (February 2018) Retrieved from https://www.smithsonianmag.com/history/axeman-new-orleans-preyed-italian-immigrants-180968037/

Monroe, Heather; Unsolved: The Axeman of New Orleans (August 2019) Retrieved from https://heathermonroe.medium.com/unsolved-the-axeman-murderer-of-new-orleans-2580c0fa59b

Weiser, Kathy; Legends of America: The Axeman of New Orleans (November 2020) Retrieved from https://www.legendsofamerica.com/la-axeman/

Sawyer, Bobbie Jean; Did Billy the Kid Really Die In A Shootout? He May Have Actually Lived To 90 (January 2021) Retrieved from https://www.wideopencountry.com/billy-the-kid/

Moreno, Eric; The Old Man Who Claimed To Be Billy The Kid (March 2017) Retrieved from https://www.atlasobscura.com/articles/billy-the-kid-brushy-bill-roberts

Kiger, Patrick J.; How Did Milly The Kid Die? (May 2020) Retrieved from https://www.history.com/news/billy-the-kid-death-theories

Meier, Allison; The Lake Monsters of America (November 2013) Retrieved from https://www.atlasobscura.com/articles/map-of-american-lake-monsters

Krystek, Lee; Lake Monsters of North America (2006) Retrieved from http://www.unmuseum.org/nlake.htm

Liptak, Andrew; North American Lake Monsters Is Weird Fiction At Its Best (April 2014) Retrieved from https://gizmodo.com/north-american-lake-monsters-is-weird-horror-fiction-at-1563224295

Sweeney Gary; A Journey of Death: What Happened to Ambrose Bierce (November 2016) Retrieved from https://the-line-up.com/ambrose-bierce

Gander, Forrest; The Many Deaths Of Ambrose Bierce (October 2014) Retrieved from https://www.theparisreview.org/blog/2014/10/17/very-trustworthy-witnesses/

Melissa; Whatever Happened To Ambrose Bierce (March 2014) Retrieved from http://www.todayifoundout.com/index.php/2014/03/whatever-happened-ambrose-bierce/

Walker, John; Keep On Moving: The Bizarre Dance Epidemic Of Summer 1518 (July 2018) Retrieved from https://www.theguardian.com/stage/2018/jul/05/bizarre-dance-epidemic-of-summer-1518-strasbourg

Author Unknown; The town That Neatly Danced Itself To Death; Retrieved from https://www.bbc.com/future/article/20161028-the-town-the-nearly-danced-itself-to-death

Andrews, Evan; What Was The Dancing Plague of 1518? (March 2020) Retrieved from https://www.history.com/news/what-was-the-dancing-plague-of-1518

Roblin Sebastian; In 1871, America 'Invaded' Korea. Here's What Happened. (January 2018) Retrieved from https://nationalinterest.org/blog/the-buzz/1871-america-invaded-korea-heres-what-happened-24113

Graham, Jed; US Invasion of Korea – 1871 (May 2020) Retrieved from https://historyofyesterday.com/u-s-invasion-of-korea-1871-5755b375a458

Wikipedia; United States Expedition To Korea (July 2021) Retrieved from https://en.wikipedia.org/wiki/United_States_expedition_to_Korea

Rohrer, Finlo; Who is the 'Barefoot Bandit'? (July 2010) Retrieved from https://www.bbc.com/news/10543769

Unknown Author; Barefoot Bandit; Retrieved from https://www.crimemuseum.org/crime-library/robberies/barefoot-bandit/

Wayking, Slone; What Type of Moth Does Not Have A Mouth? Retrieved from https://animals.mom.com/type-moth-not-mouth-10864.html

Author Unknown; Why Do Luna Moths Not Have Mouths? (May 2021) Retrieved from https://everythingwhat.com/why-do-luna-moths-not-have-mouths

Author Unknown; 5 Cool Things You Didn't Know About Moths (But Should) (July 2013) Retrieved from https://www.nature.org/en-us/about-us/where-we-work/united-states/5-cool-things-you-didnt-know-about-moths/

Andrei, Mihai; Meet Unsinkable Sam: The Cat That Survived Three Ships Sinking In WWII (May 2021) Retrieved from https://www.zmescience.com/other/feature-post/unsinkable-sam-cat-wwii/

Wikipedia; Unsinkable Sam (July 2021) Retrieved from https://en.wikipedia.org/wiki/Unsinkable_Sam

Golder, Andy; 12 Truly Weird Historical Events That Actually Happened (September 2019) Retrieved from https://www.buzzfeed.com/andyneuenschwander/12-truly-weird-historical-events-that-actually-happ

Carlson, Brady; Ernest Hemingway's Brother Tried to Make Half Of A Raft Into A Country (July 2021) Retrieved from https://www.bradycarlson.com/ernest-hemingways-brother-tried-to-make-half-of-a-raft-into-a-country-cool-weird-awesome-578/

Katz, Jason; In Miami Ernest's Brother Les Hemingway Founded a Micronation, Hosted Seances, and Hunted Nazis (June 2021) Retrieved from https://www.miaminewtimes.com/news/a-profile-of-leicester-les-hemingway-and-his-new-atlantis-micronation-12385490

Clark, Laura; The Great Goldfish Swallowing Craze of 1939 Never Really Ended (February 2015) Retrieved from https://www.smithsonianmag.com/smart-news/great-goldfish-swallowing-craze-1939-180954429/

Unknown Author; Goldish Swallowing; Retrieved from http://www.badfads.com/goldfish-swallowing/

Kruse, Colton; College Bros In The 1930s Were The Champs Of Goldfish Swallowing (February 2018) Retrieved from https://www.ripleys.com/weird-news/goldfish-swallowing/

Wikipedia; Ronal Reagan Speaks Out Against Socialized Medicine (January 2021) Retrieved from https://en.wikipedia.org/wiki/Ronald_Reagan_Speaks_Out_Against_Socialized_Medicine

Roy, Avik; Ronald Regan's Advice On Health Reform (February 2011) Retrieved from https://www.forbes.com/sites/theapothecary/2011/02/06/ronald-reagans-advice-on-health-reform/?sh=4b4877a99a8f

Flatley, Louise; The Bizarre Obsessive-Compulsive Rituals and Habits of Nikola Tesla (November 2018) Retrieved from https://www.thevintagenews.com/2018/11/22/nikola-teslas-ocd/

Kelly, Kevin; Everything You Need To Know About The Madness of Nikola Tesla (January 2008) Retrieved from https://gizmodo.com/everything-you-need-to-know-about-the-madness-of-nikola-349473

Staff Writers; 10 Incredible Real-Life Mad Scientists (April 2021) Retrieved from https://www.bestcollegereviews.org/10-incredible-real-life-mad-scientists/

Agarwal, Ishita; The Forgotten Olympic Art Competitions (November 2020) retrieved from https://historicallyspeakingssc.wordpress.com/2020/11/19/the-forgotten-olympic-art-competitions/

Wikipedia; Art Competitions at the Summer Olympics (July 2021) Retrieved from https://en.wikipedia.org/wiki/Art_competitions_at_the_Summer_Olympics

Fetters, Ashley; Remember When the Olympics Used to Have an Art Competition? No? (July 2012) Retrieved from https://www.theatlantic.com/entertainment/archive/2012/07/remember-when-the-olympics-used-to-have-an-art-competition-no/260355/

Stromberg, Joseph; When the Olympics Gave Out Medals for Art (July 2012) Retrieved from https://www.smithsonianmag.com/arts-culture/when-the-olympics-gave-out-medals-for-art-6878965/

Just Annet; Ketchup Was Sold as Medicine in the 1800s (March 2021) Retrieved from https://historyofyesterday.com/ketchup-was-sold-as-medicine-in-the-1800s-8b601329bc28

Suzanne; Ketchup Was Once Used As Medicine (January 2017) Retrieved from https://www.ripleys.com/weird-news/ketchup-was-once-used-as-medicine/

Mediratta, Sanira; Tomato Ketchup Was Once Sold As A Medicine (February 2017) Retrieved from https://inshorts.com/en/news/tomato-ketchup-was-once-sold-as-a-medicine-1487850469245#:~:text=Tomato%20ketchup%20was%20once%20sold%20as%20a%20medicine&text=In%20the%201830s%2C%20tomato%20ketchup,form%20of%20'tomato%20pills'.

Bell, Emily; That Time Russia Ran Out of Vodka (February 2016) Retrieved from https://www.foodandwine.com/drinks/time-russia-ran-out-vodka

Budnik, Ruslan; Russia Ran Out of Vodka Celebrating the End of WW2, They Showed the World How To Party (January 2019) Retrieved from https://www.warhistoryonline.com/instant-articles/the-day-of-victory-vodka.html

The Mag; The Time Russia Ran Out of Vodka (April 2012) Retrieved from https://www.mentalfloss.com/article/30351/time-russia-ran-out-vodka

Lewis, Dan; Thomas Edison Drove the Film Industry to California (July 2016) Retrieved from https://www.mentalfloss.com/article/51722/thomas-edison-drove-film-industry-california

O'Brien, Garret; Thomas Edison: The Unintentional Founder of Hollywood (March 2021) Retrieved from https://www.saturdayeveningpost.com/2021/03/thomas-edison-the-unintentional-founder-of-hollywood/

Braswell, Sean; Thomas Edison and Hollywood's Sordid Start (March 2014) Retrieved from https://www.ozy.com/true-and-stories/thomas-edison-and-hollywoods-sordid-start/1427/

Tarazano, D. Lawrence; People Feared Being Buried Alive So Much That They Invented These Special Safety Coffins (October 2018) Retrieved from https://www.smithsonianmag.com/sponsored/people-feared-being-buried-alive-so-much-they-invented-these-special-safety-coffins-180970627/

Lalani, Shiraz; Gruesome Origins of 16 Everyday Phrases From 'Saved By The Bell' to 'Gone to Pot' (August 2013) Retrieved from https://www.mirror.co.uk/news/uk-news/gruesome-origins-everyday-phrases-saved-2154388

Author Unknown; The True Origin Of The Phrase "Saved By The Bell"; Retrieved from https://theuijunkie.com/saved-by-the-bell-origin/

McNearney, Allison; The French Built a Fake Paris to Fool German Bombers in World War One (December 2017) Retrieved from https://www.thedailybeast.com/the-french-built-a-fake-paris-to-fool-german-bombers-in-world-war-one?ref=scroll

Heichelbech, Rose; Secrets from a Century Ago – The Fake Paris You Never Knew About (2021) Retrieved from https://dustyoldthing.com/wwi-secret-fake-paris/

Cuttle, Jade; A 'Second Paris' Was Built During WWI To Confuse German Bombers (March 2018) Retrieved from https://theculturetrip.com/europe/france/paris/articles/a-second-paris-was-built-during-wwi-to-confuse-german-bombers/

Wikipedia; Francis Crick (July 2021) Retrieved from https://en.wikipedia.org/wiki/Francis_Crick

Author Unknown; Francis Crick, the Detective of Life (June 2016) Retrieved from https://www.bbvaopenmind.com/en/science/bioscience/francis-crick-the-detective-of-life/

Oleksinski, Johnny; This Sex-Crazed Cultist Was The Father of Modern Rocketry (June 2018) Retrieved from https://nypost.com/2018/06/19/this-sex-crazed-cultist-was-the-father-of-modern-rocketry/

Solon, Olivia; Occultist Father of Rocketry 'Written Out" of NASA History (April 2014) Retrieved from https://www.wired.co.uk/article/jpl-jack-parsons

Lin, Alex; The Occultist History Behind NASA's Jet Propulsion Laboratory (November 2020) Retrieved from https://www.supercluster.com/editorial/the-occult-history-behind-nasas-jet-propulsion-laboratory

Fox, Dan; Strange Angel: How Rocket Scientist and Occultist Jack Parsons Laid The Foundations for Space Travel (June 2018) Retrieved

223

from https://www.frieze.com/article/strange-angel-how-rocket-scientist-and-occultist-jack-parsons-laid-foundations-space-travel

Edwards, Phil; Tesla Vs. Edison – And What the Never-Ending Battle Says About Us (July 2015) Retrieved from https://www.vox.com/2015/7/21/8951761/tesla-edison

Zakarin, Jordan; Why Thomas Edison and Nikola Tesla Clashed During the Battle of the Currents (May 2021) Retrieved from https://www.biography.com/news/thomas-edison-nikola-tesla-feud

Unknown Author; Tesla versus Edison: The Conflict That Have Us Alternating Current (October 2019) Retrieved from https://www.endesa.com/en/blogs/endesa-s-blog/others/tesla-edison-war

Valciulaityte, Giedre; Here are 30 Of The Most Ridiculous Facts In History (July 2020) Retrieved from https://www.boredpanda.com/weird-ridiculous-history-facts/?all_submissions=true&media_id=2088851&utm_source=google&utm_medium=organic&utm_campaign=organic

Liles, Maryn; 125 Mind-Blowing Historic Facts & Trivia That Are Almost Too Weird To Be True (October 2020) Retrieved from https://parade.com/1099930/marynliles/history-facts/

Weller, Chris; 10 Bizarre Historical Events That Would Break The Internet If They Happened Now (May 2016) Retrieved from https://www.businessinsider.com/weird-historical-events-that-would-break-the-internet-2016-5

Vitelli, Dr. Romeo; Dr. John Wilkins: Reaching for the Moon in the 17th Century (November 2017) Retrieved from https://brewminate.com/dr-john-wilkins-reaching-for-the-moon-in-the-17th-century/

Royal Astronomical Society (RAS); The 'Jacobean Space Progamme": Rediscovering Bishop John Wilkins (January 2014) Retrieved from https://www.sciencedaily.com/releases/2014/01/140109175549.htm

Zarrelli, Natalie; The 17th-Century Moon Mission That Never Got Off the Ground (May 2017) Retrieved from https://www.atlasobscura.com/articles/john-wilkins-moon-mission

Kelly, Lyn; The Fascinating Truth Behind Mary's Little Lamb (July 2019) Retrieved from https://www.history101.com/truth-behind-mary-little-lamb/

Amelinckx, Andrew; The True Story Behind "Mary Had a Little Lamb" (December 2017) Retrieved from https://modernfarmer.com/2017/12/true-story-behind-mary-little-lamb/

Eschner, Kat; 'Mary Had a Little Lamb's Based on a True Story (May 2017) Retrieved from https://www.smithsonianmag.com/smart-news/mary-had-little-lamb-based-true-story-180963330/

Chan, Szu Ping; When Pepsi Was Swapped for Soviet Warships (June 2019) Retrieved from https://www.bbc.com/news/business-48343589

Nambi, Karthick; When Pepsi Had The 6th Largest Navy in the World (September 2019) Retrieved from https://medium.com/history-in-bytes/when-pepsi-had-6th-largest-navy-in-the-world-4612708b70d2

Kirkpatrick, Tim; How Pepsi Briefly Became the 6th Largest Military In The World (July 2018) Retrieved from https://www.businessinsider.com/how-pepsi-briefly-became-the-6th-largest-military-in-the-world-2018-7

Unknown Author; The Whiskey War on Hans Island You Must Know; Retrieved from https://usaspiritsratings.com/en/blog/insights-1/the-whisky-war-on-hans-island-you-must-know-96.htm

Levin, Dan; Canada and Denmark Fight Over Island With Whisky and Schnapps (November 2016) Retrieved from https://www.nytimes.com/2016/11/08/world/what-in-the-world/canada-denmark-hans-island-whisky-schnapps.html

Annetts Kailie; Canada's 30 Year War With Denmark Has Finally Come To An End And The Story Is So F*cking Canadian (May 2018) Retrieved from https://www.narcity.com/toronto/canadas-30-year-war-with-denmark-has-finally-come-to-an-end-and-story-is-so-fucking-canadian

Remakant, Manu; The Tipping Point: How Bottles, Not Bullets Are Used in This Peculiar war Between Canada & Denmark on Hans Island (March 2020) Retrieved from https://www.news18.com/news/lifestyle/food-the-tippling-point-how-bottles-not-bullets-are-used-in-this-peculiar-war-between-canada-denmark-on-hans-island-2537279.html

Adhikari, Somak; Tsutomu Yamaguchi, The Man Who Survived Both Hiroshima And Nagasaki Atomic Bombings (August 2020) Retrieved from https://www.indiatimes.com/news/world/tsutomu-yamaguchi-the-man-who-survived-both-hiroshima-and-nagasaki-atomic-bombings-519925.html

Nweke, Benjamin; The Man Who Survived Two Atomic Bombs (February 2020) Retrieved from https://medium.com/lessons-from-history/the-man-who-survived-two-atomic-bombs-c11281662ea0

Andrew, Evan; The Man Who Survived Two Atomic Bombs (August 2018) Retrieved from https://www.history.com/news/the-man-who-survived-two-atomic-bombs

Keith; Violet Jessop: Irish-Argentine Traveller & Titanic Survivor (June 2021) Retrieved from https://nomadflag.com/violet-jessop/

Simonovski, Nikola; Violet Jessop: The Nurse Who Survived All Three Disasters Aboard Sister Ships: The Titanic, Britannic and Olympic (April 2017) Retrieved from https://www.thevintagenews.com/2017/04/13/violet-jessop-the-nurse-who-survived-all-three-disasters-aboard-the-sister-ships-the-titanic-britannic-and-olympic/

Mahoney, Kayla; Violet Jessop: The World's Most Unsinkable Woman (September 2019) Retrieved from https://museumhack.com/violet-jessop/

Acknowledgements

This is a special thanks to the following history lovers who have taken time out of their busy schedule to be part of History Compacted Launch Team. Thank you all so much for all the feedbacks and support. Let's continue our journey to simplify the stories of history!

Steve Thomson, Bill Anderson, Karol Pietka, David Ball, Patricia King, Janel Iverson, Dave Kaiser, Joshua Sargent, Tom Daley, Axel Andersen, Christian Loucq, Janalyn Prude Bergeron, Amanda Kliebert, Ellen M Martin, Anthony Rodriguez, Ricky Burk, Rick Conley, Holli-Marie Taylor, Charity Voskuil, Ray Workman, Judy Kirkbride, Kim Lyon, Ronald Macaulay, Simon Hardy, Casey Bates, Joan Johnson, Maryann Mahan, Matthew Peters, Kevin Gilhooly, Charles Hallett, John Eustis

About History Compacted

Here in History Compacted, we see history as a large collection of stories. Each of these amazing stories of the past can help spark ideas for the future. However, history is often proceeded as boring and incomprehensible. That is why it is our mission to simplify the fascinating stories of history.

Visit Us At: www.historycompacted.com

Dark Minds In History

For updates about new releases, as well as exclusive promotions, sign up for our newsletter and you can also receive a free book today. Thank you and see you soon.

Sign up here: https://freebook.historycompacted.com/

HISTORY COMPACTED

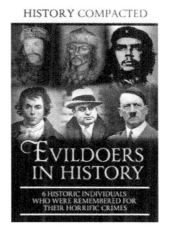

Evildoers in History: 6 Historic Individuals Remembered For Their Horrific Crimes is a book that explores the stories of six infamous criminals in history, these evildoers were not remembered by their countless murders but by the brutality with which they took the lives of their victims. There is no other term to describe them but ruthless, as you will soon find out.

Prepare yourself, the gruesome part of history is not for everyone...

Printed in Great Britain
by Amazon